Running with Lydiard

Photos with kind support of

Arthur Lydiard/ Garth Gilmour

Running with Lydiard

Meyer & Meyer Sport

British Library Cataloguing in Publication Data
A catalogue record for this book is available from the British Library

Lydiard/Gilmour:
Running with Lydiard/Lydiard/Gilmour.
- Oxford : Meyer & Meyer Sport (UK) Ltd., 2000
ISBN 1-84126-026-6

© 2000 by Meyer & Meyer Sport (UK) Ltd
Oxford, Aachen, Olten (CH), Vienna,
Québec, Lansing/Michigan, Adelaide, Auckland, Johannesburg, Budapest
 Member of the World
Sportpublishers Association
Photos: Neil's Shipper
Cover photo: Neil's Shipper
Cover design: Susanne Dalley, Aachen
Cover and Type exposure: frw, Reiner Wahlen, Aachen
Editorial: Dr. Irmgard Jaeger, Aachen
E-mail: verlag@meyer-meyer-sports.com
Printed and bound in Germany by
Druckpunkt Offset GmbH, Bergheim
ISBN 1-84126-026-6

Contents

Introduction

In 1961, in the foreword to *Run to the Top*, the first book Arthur LYDIARD and I wrote together, I said he was one of the outstanding athletic coaches of all time.

Twenty-one years later, when we produced *Running with Lydiard*, an updated sequel, I wrote that it was now doubtful if there would ever be another coach who would even equal the impact Lydiard had made on physical conditioning as a prerequisite to sporting achievement in any field and as a way of life for millions of happy joggers and fun runners.

Now, thirty-nine years later, there is no room for doubt. LYDIARD´S training and conditioning methods have not been bettered. They have not been equalled. They have become, in one form or another, the training basis of virtually every successful athlete in the last quarter of this century – the variation being that the more complete the adoption of the LYDIARD way, the higher the degree of success is likely to have been.

Arthur LYDIARD, who was unknown when his athletes astounded the world by winning three medals at the 1960 Olympic Games in Rome – Murray HALBERG (5,000 metre gold), Peter SNELL (800 metre gold) and Barry MAGEE (marathon bronze) – is an international athletic and physical fitness icon without peer.

Now in his eighties, he still has the magical combination of conditioning savvy, peaking expertise and psychological understanding and encouragement which enables him to take any average athlete and, with that athlete's faith and full co-operation, produce an outstanding sports achiever.

LYDIARD, for half a century, has made his methods freely available to anyone who wants to use them and his system has been applied, with success, to the conditioning of football players, cyclists, canoeists and kayakers, squash players, gridiron footballers, triathletes and duathletes, pentathletes, tennis players ... the list goes on. It has a place in every sporting activity because its fundamental aim is to build a high level of basic fitness on which the specific skills of any sports can be balanced.

The millions who were caught in the world-wide flood of interest in jogging, which LYDIARD and friends launched in New Zealand in 1962, can testify that the same fitness basis has contributed to improved work performance, to better sleep patterns, to greater interest in everyday activities and, if not to longer life, then to greatly enhanced enjoyment of the later years when, in the past, people began looking downhill all the way to the cemetery.

The story of LYDIARD'S evolvement of his revolutionary training method has been told many times but its bare bones bear repeating because they explain how thorough was his research into perfecting it. At the outset, he did not plan to become a champion; he had no intention of producing champions; he had no idea of changing the way the running world approached training methods. He was merely concerned, in 1945, that he was not as fit as he thought he should be as a football player and occasional and sometimes successful runner. He worried about what he might be like in another decade or two if he did not change his casual and haphazard training, if he continued to kid himself he was fit when he knew he was not.

His experiment to raise his own level of fitness lasted for ten years. He returned to active athletics to measure his progress and, at an age where everyone else was convinced they were too old, became a scratch runner over three miles, a provincial cross-country representative and a contender for national titles. His early competition results revealed flaws in his training so he continued flogging himself through slowly-evolving patterns of exercise until, gradually, the final basic theory emerged – that long, even-paced running at a strong speed produced increasing strength and endurance, even when it was continued close to the point of collapse, and that it was benefical, not harmful, to regular competition because it enabled the easy absorption of intense speed and strength training later.
    Compulsion drove him to further refinements. He battered himself over steep country runs up to 50 kms, determined to find the limits of human endurance and, within it, the formula for successful competitive running. He was growing older but he was growing fitter so he turned to the marathon and found that by training for marathons he could run even faster on the track. The key was in his hand.

Along the way, he had caught the attention and then the faithful dedication of a number of young runners who lived in his neighbourhood. They shared his enthusiasm and were inspired by his intensity and convictions and, when one of those early pupils, after trailing LYDIARD on his runs for two years, whipped a provincial championship field by 80 metres – a gap he established in the first lap – LYDIARD was established as a coach. The lad, Lawrie KING, went on to be a New Zealand cross-country champion, a six-mile record-holder and a 1954 Commonwealth and Empire Games representative.

LYDIARD was by then his country's top marathon runner and more people were taking notice of the sophistication and challenge he was bringing to a race long regarded as the occupation of mental deficients.

When, in 1957, he finally retired from competitive running, one of his motley following of youngsters was Murray HALBERG. LYDIARD had predicted in 1953 that he would become the finest middle distance runner New Zealand had known, Jack LOVELOCK included, and, although few then believed him and quite a lot laughed at him, he was right. Seven years after LYDIARD made the claim, HALBERG thrashed the world in the Olympic 5,000 metres and went on to become a sub-four minute miler and world record breaker. He, SNELL and MAGEE raced themselves to fame and their coach to immortality.

From then on, LYDIARD was in demand all over the world and he is still, in his eighties, a key figure at coaching seminars and as a motivator and mentor of men, women and children in all kinds of sporting activity. He no longer chooses to coach athletes but cannot resist when youngsters with signs of promise approach him for help; in recent years, he has scored national and international succes with many of them.

He has just sent a young girl out on the same journey that he plotted for HALBERG, SNELL and company away back in the fifties. Fresh from a cross-country win in Auckland, New Zealand, she was asked by LYDIARD if she was prepared to spend three months, as they had done more than once, running a minimum of 160 km a week to take that vital step upward in physical condition which would be her launch-pad for even greater success. He had not yet determined what distances she would prove best at but he knew that, if she put in the effort, she would excel at it. Unhesitatingly, she accepted the challenge because, like many before her, she also accepted that what Arthur LYDIARD said would happen most probably if she followed his regime.

So we come back to what I said earlier. The past has established, without question, that Arthur LYDIARD is the best distance coach the world has ever known. I believe the future will establish that he will never be eclipsed.

Garth Gilmour
Auckland 1999

1.   The Physiology of Exercise

When we wrote *Run to the Top*, the world of running was comparatively small. Jogging, the exercise form which has since turned millions into runners, was about to take off. I had not then delved deeply into physiology as it applied to athletic performance; nor, in fact, was the significance of it as an explanation of, and a guide to, athletic effort widely understood or even under investigation.

Since then, I have been able to add several years of lay study of physiology in conjunction with physiologists and sports medicine institutes to my 48 years' practical experience as an athlete and coach. It is still impossible to be explicit or exact about the physiological reactions of hard training because, whoever and however many we study, every athlete is a distinct individual with subtly different reactions. But what we have learnt, and are still learning every day, is enough to enable us to lay down, with considerable accuracy, training parameters or guidelines which will help to bring you to maximum efficiency as an athlete.

Fundamentally, my training system is based on a balanced combination of aerobic and anaerobic running. Aerobic running means within your capacity to use oxygen – everyone, according to his or her physical condition, is able to use a limited amount of oxygen each minute. The limit is raised by the proper exercise.

We call the limit the maximum steady state; the level at which you are working to the limit of your ability to breathe in, transport and use oxygen. When you exercise beyond that maximum steady state, your running becomes anaerobic. Chemical changes occur in your body's metabolism to supply the oxygen you need to supplement what you can breathe in, transport and use. It is a reconversion process with strict limits – again extendable to a known maximum by balanced exercise – so the body is always limited in its anaerobic capacity.

The reaction that takes place to sustain anaerobic running is called 'oxygen debt'. It can be incurred quickly and is accompanied by the accumulation of lactic acid and other waste products which lead directly to neuromuscular breakdown or, simply, tired muscles that refuse to continue to work as you want them to. That absolute limit when you are exercising anaerobically is an oxygen debt of 15 to 18 litres a minute; but that is a level that the average athlete will not reach until he or she has exercised properly and for long enough.

One feature of the oxygen debt is that, as you run into it, it doubles, squares and cubes. As the speed of running is raised, the oxygen requirement increases with dramatic speed.

MOREHOUSE and MILLER´S *The Physiology of Exercise* records these figures to show the effect:

Yards a second	Litres a minute
5.56 to 6.45 — An increase of .89 yards a second	5.08 to 8.75 — An increase in oxygen requirement of 3.67
9.10 to 9.23 — An increase of .13 yards a second	28.46 to 33.96 — An increase in oxygen requirement of 5.5

MOREHOUSE and MILLER have also shown that aerobic exercise is 19 times more economical than anaerobic. The more intense the exercise becomes, the faster and less economically the body's fuel is used and the faster the lactic acid forms.

Having established the basic fundamental of my training system, let us look more closely at the running body. It is not just a matter of working muscles; exercise requires continuing adjustments in respiration, chemical reactions, circulation, temperature-regulating mechanisms, kidney functions and so on. The entire body is involved and affected when you run - one of the reasons why running is such a fine general conditioner.

The effect of lactic acid in the bloodstream is to alter the blood pH - the measure of the blood's degree of alkalinity or acidity. The neutral point between these two conditions is 7.0 and normal blood pH is between 7.46 and 7.48, or slightly alkaline. Under severe physical tests and hard anaerobic exercise, however, the increase in acidity can lower the level, in extreme cases, to 6.8 or 6.9 and, if it stays at that level, the nutritive system is upset, which destroys or neutralises the benefits of food vitamins and retards general development. The pH range within which vitamins function is small, so any prolonged lowering of the level can be damaging. Enzyme functions are adversely affected, so recovery from training is poor and subsequent training becomes more difficult. A continued lowered pH level can also affect the central nervous system, causing loss of sleep and irritability and, consequently, a lessening of interest in training and competing. This is a physiological reaction which can become seriously psychological. Blood platelets are reduced in number and the athlete is more susceptible to injury and illness because immunity is weakened.

Your general efficiency and ultimate results in running depend basically on your ability to absorb oxygen from the air, transport it to various muscles and organs and then use it. Most people take into their lungs far more oxygen than they can use because they lack the necessary blood tone and blood flow from the heart to the lungs to assimilate it. Their deficiency, normally, is in haemoglobin, the pigment in the blood's red cells which combines with oxygen to transport it.

The aerobic section of my training system is directed towards improving the efficiency of these factors. Through aerobic conditioning, the heart, which is just another muscle, becomes bigger and improves its ability: it pumps more blood with each contraction and is also able to pump faster. During rest, your heart pumps about four litres of blood a minute but it can increase its capacity eight or ten times, according to your condition. An athlete who runs daily for long periods maintains a reasonably high pressure on the blood circulatory system and steadily develops better circulation and the ability to transport greater volumes of blood to various parts of the body.

This steady work and continued pressure progressively improve pulmonary ventilation – the periodic renewal of air in the lungs. The lungs are thus more efficient, with increased pulmonary capillary bed activity which enables the better-toned blood flowing through the system to absorb more oxygen more easily and faster. In conjunction with this lung development, the generally raised pressure of the blood flow is expanding the arterial and general circulatory system. Muscles have been scientifically photographed to show that in athletes and manual workers, the arterial network is clearly defined with many well-developed channels for blood circulation; in sedentary workers, particularly those who take little exercise, the development is limited and fast, thorough blood circulation is impossible.

Continued use of muscles for long periods actually develops new capillaries within the muscles, all of which increases the efficiency with which oxygen can be distributed to working muscles and used, and waste products eliminated. All these factors lead to the fine state of endurance we are seeking through aerobic exercise.

One consequence of the general improvement is that the heart begins to do its work more easily, which is reflected by a progressive decrease in the basic pulse rate. This rate is influenced by many factors – posture, emotion, body temperature, exercise and stress – so it is difficult to use it as an exact guide to fitness and it is misleading to compare rates between athletes because the normal at-rest heart rate can vary from 50 to 90 beats a minute.

However, whatever your normal pulse rate may be, you will observe that, if it is taken at rest under similar conditions from time to time, there is a steady drop in the beats a minute. The rate eventually can decrease as much as 25 beats a minute.

The youngsters of 15, 14 and even younger who regularly achieve new swimming records these days are a perfect example of how this aerobic endurance theory works. They can outswim mature people to these marks because they can do a great deal of long, slow aerobic swimming in training, their light bodies combining with water buoyancy to make them almost weightless. They use their muscles only to propel themselves along; if they had also to lift their body weight against gravity, they would not do so well. They are also able to use oxygen more efficiently than adults in comparison with their body weight. They do not become strong in the sense that they could lift heavy weights but they can continue swimming at comparatively fast speeds for long periods without experiencing muscle tiredness.

I learnt years ago when I was averaging 24 kilometres a day in training that if I shifted the daily balance to 32 kilometres one day and 16 kilometres the next, I got better reactions without altering my total running distance. Simply, the longer runs developed that greater muscular endurance; the shorter ones provided recovery and consolidation.

Years later, at Cologne University in West Germany, physiologists experimenting with endurance athletes proved that if muscle groups are exercised continually for long periods – particularly for periods of two hours or more – fine muscular endurance is attained. They established that this was directly due to the expansion of neglected capillary beds and the formation of entirely new ones to improve oxygen transportation and use.

Runners with a two-hour programme for the day often ask if it is all right to split the two hours into two one-hour sessions. My answer always is that continued exercise is the key, so two short periods will not be nearly as effective as one long one.

This is an argument often used by LSD (long slow distance) runners to support their style of training. I agree that they will gain from their system of long slow runs lasting several hours, but they will not get the best results – the aerobic pressure must be kept up to near the maximum steady state and, with increasing fitness, that level rises so the exercise must increase in pressure with it. A level of aerobic effort between 70 and 100 percent in training is most effective for the time spent running and the LSD system does not reach that.

Now, while aerobic exercise in volume will develop fine general cardiac efficiency, or a higher maximum steady state, it is also necessary to develop the capacity to exercise anaerobically, to increase the body's ability to withstand maximum oxygen debts. This means that, as part of your training, you have to create fatigue levels which will stimulate your body metabolism to react against them.

This metabolic activity can compensate for lack of oxygen up to a limit, as we have stated, of 15 to 18 litres a minute. At this level, neuromuscular breakdown – or complete exhaustion of the muscle – can be withheld until the lactic acid concentration is as high as 200 mg to 100 ml of blood.

For example, if a runner has a steady state of three litres a minute, can sustain a 15-litre debt and the workload he or she is performing requires four litres a minute, the effort can be maintained for 15 minutes – using one litre of debt capacity each minute. If the workload is increased to five litres a minute, the runner will maintain the effort for only 7 $\frac{1}{2}$ minutes because the rate at which the debt capacity is used is doubled to two litres a minute. Every runner knows that if he or she sprints at full effort, no great distance is achieved compared with what can be run if the effort and speed are lowered. This is determined by aerobic capacity.

The critical factors are the extent, intensity and regularity with which you subject yourself to fatigue levels in training. Many training programmes are based on this broad principle but many coaches and athletes go to extremes to create oxygen debts in the hope that, by doing so, the body's metabolism will be overstimulated into developing more general efficiency against fatigue. They try to hurry and concentrate the process, forgetting that anaerobic exercise is always uneconomic and that, when fatigue rates are created, the body must be allowed conditions in which to recover before further fatiguing effort is applied.

When the maximum steady state, the aerobic exercise upper level, is low, you can be running anaerobically at a comparatively low speed; as the maximum steady state is pushed upwards, the slower anaerobic speeds become aerobic (and economical). And, if training progresses on this principle – that aerobic exercise is 19 times more economical than anaerobic – then the possibilities of running farther and faster aerobically (and with economy) must increase.

The daily programme of sustained aerobic running is absolutely essential to achieve the correct respiratory and circulatory development and the longer the periods of running the better the results will be. The anaerobic section of your preparation should be tackled only after you have developed aerobic capacity and maximum steady state to the highest possible level; then it must be fairly extreme for a defined period to develop a matching high anaerobic capacity. At this point, you will be aiming to create a big oxygen debt and lower your pH level so that your metabolism is stimulated to build buffers against fatigue. Once you have built those buffers to maximum efficiency, it is pointless and even risky to go on with this fatiguing training.

Four to five weeks is usually enough. You may need less. Those weeks will involve going hard for, say, three days to lower the pH, lightly training for a day to let it come up again to near normal and then pulling it down again with anaerobic effort the next day. Let it come up, pull it down again. Keep it fluctuating. If you keep it low you upset the entire system.

My most frequent admonition to athletes and coaches is: **Train, Don't Strain**. Bill BOWERMAN quoted this phrase to support his LSD training theories but, as far as I am concerned, it applies more accurately to running at faster aerobic speeds than are implied by LSD. East German physiologists have proved my contention that it is better to do the long aerobic running at between 70 and 100 percent of your maximum steady state. Lower aerobic effort, while it may be fine for joggers and fun runners, does not exert the desirable pressures on the cardiac and respiratory systems that an athlete needs.

BOWERMAN has also maintained that overtraining can result in staleness and loss of interest and, though he has not exactly defined staleness, suggests that the ideal solution is regular competition. I see staleness as a physiological reaction, caused by excessive anaerobic work, which becomes psychological through the effects of the continual low pH levels on the central nervous system. Regular competitive racing will not cure that.

I have not seen loss of interest in athletes who train aerobically over varied courses. It is not usual for them to experience problems in maintaining 160 kilometres a week of steady state aerobic running throughout the conditioning period. And when they move into the anaerobic phase, when the physiological problems could again be encountered, they are at such a level of cardiac efficiency they can handle the constant lowering and raising of the pH level without that side-effect of staleness.

As a practical example, assume we have conditioned runner A to use three litres of oxygen a minute and runner B to use five litres. We then give them the same volume and intensity of anaerobic training. Because his or her maximum state is lower, runner A will level off and begin to lose form, fighting a progressively larger oxygen debt effect; runner B will continue to hold best form. He or she can use oxygen more effectively and for longer periods.

Given that example, it is easy to see how the physiological effect on A can become a psychological problem – he or she is never going to beat B and knows it without going back to basics and building the maximum steady state higher.

If we set these two off the same mark in a 1,500-metre race, they will be together at the end of the first lap and neither will be feeling any strain because neither is yet running anaerobically. But, by the time they are into the third lap, because of the simple mathematical fact that A's capacity to use oxygen is only 3/5ths that of B, A will be feeling the pace – building an oxygen debt rapidly to keep up with B. Lactic acid is accumulating, neuromuscular breakdown is on the way. When B fires in a finishing burst up the last straight, A will not be there.

Now, if A's physiological inferiority has also become a psychological one, he or she is in real trouble before even starting. Which of the two do you want to be?

One of the greatest difficulties I have had in persuading coaches and athletes to accept my system is that the majority have been chained to the principles of interval training, which emphasises anaerobic interval training or repetition work as the MOST important phase of a training programme. As far as I am concerned, it is the LEAST important.

Anaerobic capacity can be developed to its maximum very easily with various types of work which do not need to be rigidly controlled; it is simply a matter of the athletes tiring themselves with anaerobic exercise and stopping when they feel they have had enough. If they sprinted as fast as possible, they would probably not cover more than 135 metres before their bodies were forced to compensate; if they sprinted a little slower, they could go a distance farther because the rate of increase of the oxygen debt slows in proportion to the reduction in the workload imposed by the running speed. Either way, they achieve the same end result.

No-one can be specific about this type of training. If we work hard enough, intensively enough and long enough, the pH level will come down and it does not need the regimented programme of specific numbers of repetition runs over specific distances in specific times with specific intervals in between. The difference is whether you control your training or your training controls you.

I defy any coach to say exactly what any one athlete should do for his or her anaerobic training. Training conditions vary constantly, the state of the athlete must vary almost from day to day. So you must use repetitions without anyone being concerned about the interval, as long as it is roughly equidistant; or the number to be run; or what times they should be run in. You can do 'ups and downs' – from 100 metres to 400 metres and back again – but this tends to be predetermined and regimented and I prefer to avoid them.

I like to keep my athletes away from the track as much as possible. I would rather find a forest trail or an area with a pleasant environment, warm them up and then run them to a tree or some kind of natural marker and jog them back. Then I let them continue until either I or they think they have had enough. We may use fartlek, employing hard sprints here and there with a series of repetitions. Anything is better than a systematic grind on a closed track. Different athletes using different methods in the same group can all come in tired from their workouts, all with a lowered pH level; each, in his or her own way, will have been developing an anaerobic capacity towards its maximum. The exercise does not matter; what is important is that athletes should understand the physiological reactions they are trying to achieve and should know when they feel they have had enough and why they feel that way. An athlete is less likely to overdo training and invite blackouts or vomiting because he or she has dragged the pH level excessively low and disrupted the central nervous system. However, it is important when developing an anaerobic capacity to exercise to run over distances of 200 metres or more for a longish period to get the pH blood level low. Short, sharp sprints will not do this. It requires volume of work as well as intensity.

Talking to coaches in Abilene, Texas, during an eightmonth tour of the United States in 1970, I mentioned that only twice in a year had I used 20 x 400-metre repetitions and then only because we were on a track which happened to be that size and they were useful in helping to develop pace judgement. At the end of my lecture, a high school coach told me he was training a bunch of young milers, the best of whom could run 4:17 and the others around 4:24. He was giving them 25 x 400-metre repetitions every Monday morning as well as their other anaerobic training and racing. Mostly, they ran the repetitions in 68-69 seconds.

I saw the coach several times later in the tour but he had nothing to say until we were at Iowa State University in Des Moines for the Drake relays at the end of my tour. When I began talking about anaerobic training, he asked if he could first relate his experiences with my suggested approach to training. He said that, eight months earlier, when he first listened to me, he decided to adopt my methods and began using long runs on his boys. He found a butte about twelve miles away and he took them over there for hill training.

The first day the 400-metre repetitions came up on the schedule, the boys, instead of lapping their usual 68-69 seconds, took 72-73 seconds. The coach's first thought was: *"Lydiard has ruined my programme"*. But, he said, he felt obliged to stick with it. When the repetitions came up again two weeks later and his boys ran no better, he thought: *"That's it; now the whole season's ruined."*

He really had no alternative at this late hour but to keep up to my system until the high school relay championships came up at Wichita. He sent his runners in without feeling very much hope – the fastest ran 4:09, the slowest 4:13 and they took the title.

The coach confessed at Iowa: *"All these years, I'd been developing great 400-metre repetition runners but they couldn't run a mile very fast. Now, they don't run repetitions very well but they sure can run fast miles."* He made the point for me a lot better than I could.

Before the 1974 Commonwealth Games in Christchurch, New Zealand, one of our top middle-distance prospects, Richard TAYLER, was not running too well. Something was obviously wrong with him, though none of us knew it was going to be ankylosing spondulitis which would shortly wreck his career and threaten to leave him a permanent cripple. (TAYLER, after years of agony, months in hospitals and the best part of his life in despair, has returned to running and, in 1980, ran 78th in the Honolulu marathon in 2:42:43.)

Anyway, to try to get him shaped up for the Games, in which he was running the 10,000 metres against the Africans and Dave Bedford and other tough company, I gave him a heavy loading of anaerobic training. We were working out on a college ground at Te Awamutu one day when a group of pupils stopped to watch.

"What's he doing"?, one asked.
"Repetitions", I explained.
They knew all about those. "How many is he going to do?"
"I don't know."
"What times is he running?"
"I'm not timing him."
They exchanged looks of disbelief. Was I supposed to be coaching one of New Zealand's best runners?
Then I asked, "How far round is this track, anyway?"
They knew then I did not know what I was talking about.
When Dick finished and joined us, they asked him, "How many did you do?"
"I didn't count them", Dick said.
"What times were you running?"
"I didn't time them."

I decided it was time to explain to these boys, before they ran off laughing, that times and numbers were unimportant. What mattered was the effect on TAYLER of what he was doing; and he knew better than I did what he wanted to do and when he had enough.

Anaerobic training is something we have to do if we intend to race well but, at the same time, we must always keep in mind that if we overdo it we lose our most essential asset, the very thing we have been building, our good condition, which determines our performance level. So, all the time you are building your capacity to exercise anaerobically, jealously guard your good condition or the whole purpose of the programme is defeated.

We all know runners who perform well early in the season and then lose form completely halfway through. Almost always, they are runners who have peaked with exacting anaerobic exercising but have then gone on with the heavy exercise. Not only is it unnecessary, it is also physiologically impossible to keep on a solid anaerobic training system throughout a season.

In anaerobic training, if you stop the workouts, you lose the capacity to train anaerobically; if you do too much, you lose good condition. You have to strike a happy balance and that is where sharpeners, or windsprints or killer-dillers, as they are sometimes known, come in. They improve sharpness, put the knife-edge on your good condition by creating just enough of an oxygen debt to stimulate your metabolism into maintaining the buffers that have been built against fatigue and which hold up your anaerobic racing level. It sounds like a critical line to run along but it is easily achieved.

Sharpeners are, simply, short (50 to 100 metres) sprints with 50 to 100-metre floats in between. If you go out and run 20 x 50-metre sprints in a total of about 2,000 metres, your leg muscles are going to be very tired because of the sudden accumulation of lactic acid and you will have lowered your pH level in the muscles you have been exercising. But you will not be generally tired. You will have been forced to stop the exercise by the refusal of the running muscles to continue them. In fact, a reading taken from the leg muscles after sharpeners and one taken from your ear lobe would give two totally different pH levels. Sharpeners are rather like push-ups: your muscles prevent your going on but, moments later, there is no general tiredness.

Used once a week, this type of training is most effective for maintaining maximum anaerobic development and can be continued indefinitely in conjunction with racing or time trials. You will find it in the schedules in this book.

Improved track times have been attributed to improved training techniques and a more enlightened, or perhaps more dedicated, approach to training. I do not entirely agree with this. Certainly, the training of athletes generally has improved but what has really brought times down so quickly was the introduction of new types of track surface. It would have been interesting to see how a runner like Peter SNELL, running at his best, would have performed on them. He would have rebounded off them really fast and could well have set marks which would be difficult to beat today. He ran his mile, 800 metres and 880 yards world records either on grass or on a roughly converted cinder speedway track – surfaces which would be at least a second a lap slower than the modern synthetic surfaces. Compare his 3:54.1 mile in 1964 with the world mark of 3:47.4 on that basis and see how much – or how little – the human improvement has been in 18 years.

In 1972, I was in Aarhus, Denmark, when the Australian Pam RYAN, one of the world's most proficient hurdlers, came there. She had not run on a synthetic track before and, first time out, she ran straight into the first hurdle, something she never did. She told me she did not realise she would gain so much from the change of track and felt immediately that if she could adjust her approach to the hurdles she could take the world record. Three days later, on a synthetic track in Poland, she did just that.

When synthetic tracks were introduced, the 5,000 metres world record immediately came down about half a minute and lots of 10,000-metre runners began running close to and even breaking Ron CLARKE´S world time. Over 100 metres, the synthetic top has been calculated to be worth about 2/10ths of a second.

If you want more proof, consider road racing times. Variations in courses and conditions make comparisons difficult, but top marathon times have not improved greatly. A lot more marathon runners get close to them, which reflects a better approach to marathon training and a whole lot more interest in marathon running.

But Derek CLAYTON ran 2:8.24 many years ago and only three have bettered it by a few seconds since. The reason is physiological. A male runner with an oxygen uptake level of around seven litres or 88 ml a kg – near the human maximum – can run aerobically around 2:12 for a marathon. If he can incur an oxygen debt of 15 to 18 litres and if he can control his pace all the way so that he runs barely into the anaerobic state for most of the distance and ekes out his debt capacity evenly from start to finish, he can pull that time down to 2:8 or 2:9. In a marathon, the opposition, the weather, the terrain all have their effect on who can run successfully to do that and achieve what I believe is the physiological maximum for a marathon.

This is where marathon running has been discovered to be such a fascinating and demanding event. The first person a runner must evaluate in a marathon is themselves. He or she must use their anaerobic capacities most economically, controlling the running so that they move just barely beyond their maximum steady state and stay there. If they run into it too quickly or too far, lactic acid will accumulate too fast for them to maintain the pace and may even stop them altogether. Most marathon runners do that when they are up against runners regarded as their superiors. They match paces, run into a big oxygen debt and then wonder why they are drifting back, unable to hold the pace. They would do better to let the good runners go and hold a pace at which they ration out the oxygen debt very slowly, banking on the chance that the others will misjudge their pace and come back. In a marathon, you are racing to your own capacity first and who you beat along the way depends very largely on how successfully you do that.

2   Marathon Conditioning Training

Since the HALBERG-SNELL-MAGEE era of the early 1960s, the main evolvement in my approach to conditioning training has been dictated by the fact that I now do not often see the athletes I am coaching, so I encourage them to train on a time basis, rather than on mileage. It has proved the wiser approach to coaching by remote control, especially for the faster athletes who, in a 25-kilometre run, would not spend as much time running as slower athletes and would, therefore, miss out on the most important aspect of conditioning – the volume of work they do.

A secondary aspect which favours the time basis is that athletes running over measured courses fairly regularly are inclined to pressure themselves into becoming competitive about it. They want to cover the course faster each time or can be tempted into trying to do so. If they just go out and run for, say, an hour and a half, with the pressure off, we seem to get better results. Keep this firmly in mind when you read this chapter and its references to training mileages and times.

If you have not done the marathon-type conditioning before, you must think deeply about it and try to understand clearly just what you are trying to achieve. You must relate the work you will be doing to the physiological changes and benefits outlined in the previous chapter and make sure you are not confused about the effects the various types of exercise will have on you. Sort the exercises into their various compartments, balance your schedule and get rid of any doubts about the approach to make during each development stage, right up to the climax of your racing season.

Tackle each stage as a separate exercise, distinct and different from all the others, though each is aimed at the same ultimate target. Only when you are positive about the physiological and mechanical aspects of your training will you develop the confidence you need in training if you are to become a champion.

The fundamental principle of training is simple, which may be why it needs repeating so often: it is to develop enough stamina to enable you to maintain the necessary speed for the full distance at which you plan to compete. Many runners throughout the world are able to run 400 metres in 46 seconds and faster; but remarkably few of them have sufficient stamina to run 800 metres in 1:44, or 52 seconds for each 400 metres. That clearly shows the part stamina plays in middle and distance training. It is absolutely vital.

Consider those relative times again – they will help you to realise just what could be achieved by the really fast runners if they concentrated on endurance development and shifted their attention to longer distances.

Peter SNELL was basically the slowest runner in the 800 metres final at both the Rome and Tokyo Olympics but he had the stamina to carry him through the heats and then sprint the last 100 metres of the final faster than any of his rivals. They were by then too tired to use their superior speed. SNELL was trained to be capable of running a fine marathon but his rivals were not. This was the advantage that enabled him to succeed; it is also the advantage you can give yourself.

Quite simply, it means putting your body into a near-tireless state so that oxygen debts are not created quickly and the ability to recover rapidly is at a high level. The stamina is best achieved among sportspeople by cross-country skiers; the best way after that is by running.

And the best running programme is to cover approximately 160 kilometres a week at just under your maximum steady state, plus any supplementary running, such as jogging, that you feel inclined or have the time to do.

When we prepared *Run to the Top* in the early 1960s, we based the stamina-building phase on this 160 kilometres a week and many runners adopted this as a no-more no-less requirement, which of course, it is not. In this connection, an Australian doctor with an interest in sports medicine once mentioned that the 160 kilometres a week was insufficient and that Australian athletes were running twice that.

He did not understand, perhaps because we had not explained it comprehensively enough, just what my athletes were doing. They were running 160 kilometres a week at their near-best aerobic effort during their evening runs and on a long-duration weekend run; but, like the Australians, they were also covering up to another 160 kilometres in much more easily paced morning and midday training sessions. My middle-distance men, SNELL and John DAVIES at that time, were running the lowest total weekly mileages but even they were covering about 250 kilometres a week.

I asked the doctor if, as a physiologist, he believed a runner could train more than 160 kilometres a week for periods of months at his best aerobic speed. He could not answer because he did not know but I had already proved for myself that no runner could do it. For years, I ran many kilometres trying to find the correct balance for my conditioning training. I knew it was as easy to overtrain as it was to undertrain in both mileage and effort. I ran from extremes of 80 kilometres a week to 500 kilometres a week at close to my best aerobic effort before settling on the 160 kilometres a week; then, when I added the slower supplementary runs at other times of the day, I found that they assisted my recovery from the long aerobic efforts and hastened the rate of my development.

Running is, without question, the best exercise for runners and, as long as we watch the degree of effort, we cannot really do too much of it. Some physiologists have maintained that, unless the pulse rate is brought up to 150 to 180 beats a minute, the athlete gains very little cardiac development. This is absolutely wrong; I have never believed it. If an athlete with a normal pulse of 50 to 60 beats a minute lifts the rate to 100, he or she must get cardiac development, so all supplementary jogging, while it may not impose the pressure on the system to the extent that maximum steady state running does, is supplying extra benefits to the cardiac system while it aids the athlete's recovery.

The long steady running that I term marathon conditioning is designed to induce a pleasant state of tiredness rather than fatigue, so that it does not interfere with the following day's programme. You should recover reasonably quickly.

So, first, you have to find your own basic capability – the starting point from which to begin lifting your maximum steady state. The best way to do this is to run an out-and-back course for, say, 30 minutes. Run out for 15 minutes at a steady pace, what you think is comfortably below your best effort; then turn and run back again, trying to maintain the pace and avoiding any forcing. If it takes you 20 minutes to get back, it shows you ran out too fast for your condition. If you are back inside 15 minutes without apparently increasing your effort, you were not running fast enough to begin with.

Next time, aim to adjust your pace according to what the first run showed you. You will run a different distance, more than or less than the first one, but you should this time come back in the same time you went out. It is good discipline and that is something you need to acquire early because you are going to need a lot more of it later.

As you learn more about yourself and improve your general physical condition, you will be able to run both farther and faster but by this time it should be ingrained in you that it is the speed of the running that stops you, not the distance you are running. Running that leaves you breathless and struggling or has you forcing yourself to keep going is anaerobic, not aerobic, and it must be avoided. It is much better to go too slowly than too fast – and if you can recognise the importance of that and discipline yourself to it, you are on your way to becoming a greater runner than you believed possible.

For the psychological reasons we have mentioned before, you should train by time rather than mileage at first. This way you do not translate your efforts into comparisons with the four-minute mile and discourage yourself by getting a quite false impression of how well you are going. Everyone has different fitness levels and backgrounds, irrespective of age or sex, so there is no hard-and-fast schedule to follow. So the early weekly schedule should incorporate three long runs, for a length of time the individual considers long according to his or her state of fitness. For instance, once the runner can handle 15 minutes a day comfortably, the routine could be: Monday 15 minutes; Tuesday 30; Wednesday 15; Thursday 30; Friday 15; Saturday 15; Sunday 30.

When this, or whatever similarly balanced schedule you elect, becomes comfortable, you gradually add time until you have reached – and you could be surprised how quickly this can be done – a schedule like this: Monday one hour; Tuesday 1 ½ hours; Wednesday one hour; Thursday two hours; Friday one hour; Saturday 2-3 hours; Sunday 1 ½ hours.

All this running must be steady and even, at a pace that leaves you tired at the end but knowing you could have run faster if you'd wanted to.

Most athletes doubt that they can run long distances day after day or even for an hour or more without stopping; particularly when they may feel extremely tired during the initial short-duration runs. It is a hurdle you must overcome if you want to improve and you can overcome it with patience and perseverance. In only a few weeks, you will find that what seemed impossible is becoming progressively easier and more enjoyable. Just do not rush it. Once you are moving freely over the shorter runs, you move into the longer runs once or twice a week to maintain the improvement rate and build confidence in yourself. You will then find it easy to slide into the schedule outlined above.

The following schedule, which is a progression again from the last one, concerns itself more with distance than time and does carry the risk that, in running measured distances over regular courses, you will begin to compete with yourself:

Monday: 15 km at $\frac{1}{2}$ effort over undulating course
Tuesday: 25 km at $\frac{1}{4}$ effort over reasonably flat course
Wednesday: 20 km at $\frac{1}{2}$ effort over hilly course
Thursday: 30 km at $\frac{1}{4}$ effort over reasonably flat course
Friday: 15 km at $\frac{3}{4}$ effort over flat course
Saturday: 35 km at $\frac{1}{4}$ effort over reasonably flat course
Sunday: 25 km at $\frac{1}{4}$ effort over any type of terrain

You need to measure a range of courses for this training, with each kilometre recorded in some way, so that you can time yourself with reasonable accuracy. They are not, however, to be used as one-kilometre pegs in a race. The effort must always be controlled.

In theory, you will now be doing a lot of running at speeds just within your maximum steady state to place the utmost safe aerobic pressure on your cardio-respiratory and cardio-vascular systems and gain the best possible progressive development. Always, however, you must finish each of your runs with the knowledge that you could have run a little faster.

If, during any of these runs, you find you have to ease back to regain rhythm and recovery of breath, you'll be warned that you have moved into the anaerobic phase. This is neither economical nor desirable. You could go on running your courses anaerobically and quite evenly for several days but then you would find yourself unable to continue because of the gradual breakdown of your entire system, so take careful note of these early warning signs and peg your speed back.

Once you have established approximately the best aerobic effort for each course, you can then cover succeeding runs to previously planned times – and this is where the discipline we mentioned earlier becomes important. The running must be strong, even and non-competitive with any other times you may have run on the same course.

You may have been under the impression that marathon type training involves slow running. This is not so, apart from the supplementary work. The top-class runners do not jog around in this phase of their preparation but run at speeds of from 3 $\frac{3}{4}$ minutes to 3 $\frac{1}{4}$ minutes a kilometre. There are still some long-distance runners who believe they should run no faster than, say, 4 $\frac{1}{4}$ minute pace and that to run faster will waste effort and produce poorer results; again, this is not so. The runners who keep their speed just within the maximum steady state will gain the same general cardiac development in far less time than the runners who train at speeds far below the maximum steady state.

In all of this, of course, it is important to bear in mind that no two of us are similar. The schedules, times and distances set out so far and later in this book are guidelines, which must be treated flexibly according to the fitness level, age and sex of the individual. And do not let age deter anyone from tackling long mileages, as long as they are happy about it and exercise carefully.

We were all inclined a decade or two ago to be cautious about allowing really young people to run long distances but we know that, as long as they are not pushed, they can cover many miles easily and beneficially. I know of boys and girls as young as ten years running up to 160 kilometres a week and improving.

Equally, there are many men and women in the senior citizen bracket who run remarkable mileages with the same ease. Their relative speeds may be totally different but their general development is much the same – all have built strong foundations of endurance.

No-one can say exactly what the limit is for any individual; each must adjust his or her running to what he or she likes and can handle comfortably, on the basis that the longer they run aerobically, the better the prospects for development are going to be.

We will look at the young runner's requirements later but I would make the point here that the black Africans have emerged as remarkably successful runners simply because running has always formed part of their daily lives. Many of them became runners because, wherever they were going, they had many miles to cover on foot, especially to and from school, and the quickest way to travel on foot was to run. It was not controlled running, beyond the discipline the youngsters might impose on themselves, but it was a vital exercise which laid the foundation for their future development as good racers. They lived nearer to nature and more perfectly than most people and developed better muscular and cardiac efficiency quite early. They became superior not because they were black but because, without knowing or working at it, they were doing more conditioning exercising than anyone else. Our children sit back in cars and buses between home and school; the Africans get there and back by running.

In 1961, the cross-country team from Victoria, Australia, came to New Zealand to compete and performed so badly they asked my athletes what was wrong. It was suggested that they should follow our system of long marathon-type running with less anaerobic work. Two of them, VINCENT and COOK, went home and began the marathon-type training with some other athletes, including Ron CLARKE, who had retired from running two years earlier but had decided to make a comeback. He had previously trained on an interval programme with lots of strenuous anaerobic track work.

Four years later, I was in Saarijarvi, Finland, when CLARKE arrived for a 3,000-metre race in which one of my runners, John DAVIES, who won the 1,500 metres bronze medal behind SNELL in Tokyo, was also running. DAVIES had not raced the distance before but, since he was marathon-trained, I was confident that, even with CLARKE in the field, he could win it. I advised him to trail CLARKE until the last 150 metres on the reasoning that CLARKE, even if he had not mentally given the race away earlier when he realised he could not get rid of Davies, would not have the finishing speed to match Davies' challenge.

That is the way it happened. DAVIES beat CLARKE quite comfortably in 7:58. Two weeks later, he ran the same distance in Czechoslovakia and comfortably beat the reigning 5,000 metres Olympic champion Bob SCHUL in 7:52. Each race was a convincing demonstration of the value of marathon-trained stamina in combination with speed development.

After the Saarijarvi race, CLARKE asked me why he showed so badly against DAVIES, why he had no speed, no kick to counter DAVIES' finishing strength. We examined his training and found that in 1961, when he joined COOK and VINCENT in the long-distance training, they ran about 7-minute mile pace (about 4 $\frac{1}{4}$ minutes a kilometre). He found he got fitter and fitter from this running until, while COOK, VINCENT and the rest continued at the same speed, he began running faster. As his steady state improved, he began running mileages he had never attempted before; by the time of the 1962 Commonwealth Games in Perth, he was fit enough to run second to Murray HALBERG in the three miles.

But CLARKE, though he did the right thing in continuing to push up his running speed as his maximum steady state increased, failed to carry the programme through to the proper conclusion to take fullest advantage of his development. He certainly ran faster but his training lacked the essential anaerobic and sprint training which would have balanced it and put the vital edge on to his racing.

On my advice, he now began to do repetition training on the track to improve his ability to exercise and race aerobically. This capitalised on his generally fine condition so quickly and effectively that, soon after Saarijarvi, he ran his fine world six miles and 10,000 metres records in Oslo.

CLARKE was a good early example of an athlete who failed to improve as he should have done with interval training, became sick of the unrewarding grind; but, once he had begun training aerobically, he not only enjoyed his running again but improved so easily that he was not prepared to revert to the type of training that had failed and discouraged him before. He had not understood that a limited injection of that tough anaerobic training was necessary to sharpen him up.

I still believe CLARKE is the best distance runner the world has yet seen but he did not balance his schedules and, for that reason, failed in many important competitions. He proved that it is not always the best athletes who win the big ones – it is the properly-prepared ones, those who are completely ready on the day.

During conditioning, all athletes have to be conscious of the difference between the development and toning of the cardiac systems and the muscular systems. Only by forcing the body weight against gravity, by using the powerful upper leg muscles and ankles, can you really make the heart work hard for long periods. Runners are lucky, they actually use all the muscles required for their sport during the conditioning stage; it is necessary only to do suppling and loosening exercises at every opportunity to round off the development. This does not and should not involve any sacrifice of running time.

The surfaces you run on are important. The better the surface and the better the traction you get from it, the better will be the development of the circulatory and respiratory systems. Good traction allows more economical, balanced running which, in turn, allows greater speed for longer periods within the maximum steady state.

It is worth nothing that skiers develop a higher maximum steady state than runners because they are using more muscles for their sport. But the circulatory development would be greater in the legs of the runner. From this, it is also interesting to note that, because more muscles are being used in skiing – arm, shoulder and back muscles play a large role – the skier's energies are expended more quickly. This also makes the point that if you do not run economically, if you use muscles not required for running (excessive arm and shoulder movement, for example), you are wasting energy in a way which will reduce the speed and the distance of your running.

Most of my runners trained on bitumen roads because they offered the best traction. We tested this by running for an hour cross-country and comparing that with the distance run in an hour on the road. On the road, a much greater distance was covered without any increase of effort, solely because the better traction allowed more economical movement without tiring the muscles so rapidly.

Cross-country is tiring because of the continued resistance of uphill and downhill running on slippery, wet or holding ground where the traction ranges from indifferent to awful. The failure is muscular, not cardiac. Even when the roads contain hills, the runner gets good traction and can run much more relaxed. General fatigue may be greater but it is no problem as long as he or she is running within the steady state; in fact, it is helping because sustained economic pressure is a better developer of the general circulatory system than the limited uneven pressures of cross-country.

Do not be afraid of training on roads. If you wear good shoes with good rubber soles, the risk of injuries or leg problems is actually less than the risk involved in running in ordinary track shoes on hard cinder tracks.

In your first year of marathon-type training, you are likely to get soreness, particularly about the knees and shins. Usually, if you continue to train carefully, the soreness vanishes. If it persists, get medical opinion. While the trouble does exist, avoid jarring the legs too much; do not run downhill fast, seek out softer surfaces for training and keep the affected areas warm.

We will discuss runners' problems more fully later but you should know that shin soreness usually stems from overstriding or running downhill too fast. Both actions cause the front of the foot to clap down hard, which jars the shin muscles and irritates the nerves and membranes between the bone and the muscles. In some cases, the muscle sheaths split.

Shorten stride and eliminate fast downhill running and you will overcome the problem, though it is not easy. Shin soreness, once you have got it, can take quite a time to recover. If you are a normally long-striding runner and susceptible to shin splints, you can counter the clapping effect by building up the forepart of your shoes with an extra half sole of rubber.

For all leg troubles, wading in cold water is excellent. It will often effect a cure where other methods fail. Ice packs also help.

You can all expect some initial troubles but none is insurmountable if commonsense and caution are applied and use is made of the best professional advice available. Most of the world's greatest athletes have had their setbacks and recovered from them.

I have emphasised relaxed running, so let us discuss what I mean. Always, during conditioning running, concentrate on being relaxed, particularly in the upper body. Keep your head up and your hips comfortably forward; it allows you to stride longer and more economically.

Never waste energy. Keep your arm action low; runners with a high arm action are not relaxed and tend to throw their torsos from side to side. They do not get over their driving legs and lose some forward momentum. It is energy down the drain.

Test yourself by running on sand or across dewy grass and then checking back on your footfalls. If you are running balanced, your feet should be on, or nearly on, a single line.

Do not run on your toes ... by which I mean, do not land on the forepart of the feet. When you are running aerobically or at low anaerobic speeds, the centre of gravity is slow getting over the leading foot, so, if you land on the forepart of the feet, you are getting too much traction on landing and actually developing a stopping motion. This can be a cause of blistered feet and shin splints.

Front of the foot running also works the calf muscles unnaturally, which is uncomfortable and tiring over a long distance. It is most economical and natural to come down with a nearly flat foot, with the heel hitting fractionally ahead of the rest of the foot and a slight roll in from the outside edge. There are runners who can run on their toes but I contend they would run better, particularly in distance work, with a nearly flat footfall.

Over 800 metres or less, of course, you do run on your toes as all sprinters do when they throw their bodies forward and go for maximum leg speed and drive. But, before you get that far, if that is your intended racing distance, you will be conditioned to do it.

Some runners seem to have rather tight or short tendons in the backs of their legs which prevent them from running heel to toe aerobically. This means that when the forward momentum is such that the centre of gravity is slow getting over the leading foot, they experience resistance in the front of the foot. These runners often have foot problems, caused through friction during high-volume aerobic running, such as blisters and metatarsal injury. They must take care to limit the movement of their feet in their shoes by lacing the shoes tightly and correctly and perhaps also by rubbing some lubricant into their feet.

3   Speed and the Anaerobic Capacity of Exercise

The phase that follows the marathon-running conditioning period is one that must be in your mind right through the initial conditioning. You should be allowing for it by doing some resistance work for the leg muscles fairly consistently and stretching your tendons for flexibility and suppleness to add to your power. Some hill springing and steep hill running should be fitted into the marathon conditioning period as an added incentive to the development of the upper leg muscles and ankles. These exercises are best included during your supplementary jogging sessions.

At the end of the marathon training you should be stacked with stamina and fairly well-toned to begin developing speed and increasing your capacity to exercise anaerobically – two elements in the programme we have been deliberately avoiding until now.

Some of you will be fortunate enough to have certain natural talents which give you advantages in different areas of endeavour; good basic speed may be one of those talents. It is a governing factor in determining what distances are going to be best for you competitively and now is the time to find out what it is. Before this, you were not fit enough to test yourself accurately; but, regardless of whether you now emerge as a prospective 800 metres, 10,000 metres or marathon runner, your conditioning programme would have been the same.

The point is that no-one and no training can make a basically slow runner into a basically fast runner. Greater speed can be developed to a limited extent in muscle toning and in general condition but the basically slow runner will remain basically slow in relation to other runners; if he or she wants to win, the choice will have to be a distance at which a lack of basic speed does not matter but at which other qualities of endurance and strength can give a reasonable prospect of success. I remind you of my earlier comment that SNELL was basically slower than most other 800-metre runners he met, and of the end results of those meetings.

Your muscles contain a number of fibres, some of them red, the others white. The red fibres contain amounts of myoglobin, which is chemically related to the haemoglobin of the blood. Muscles in which these red fibres predominate are capable of slow, powerful contractions and are not easily fatigued. The white muscle fibres contain less myoglobin and are specialised for speed, not strength, so they tire much more easily.

Runners with a good basic speed appear to have a higher ratio of white fibres to red than normal. They are born with this advantage and nothing will change it, though, through exercise and resistance training, the fibres will become larger and generally more proficient.

There are two kinds of muscle concentration – isometric and isotonic. The contraction is isotonic when the muscular effort results in movement, such as lifting an object or pushing or pulling something that moves. It is isometric when force is applied by pushing, pulling or trying to lift an immovable object. Both forms of resistance have their respective values in exercise and it is only a question of athletes and coaches evaluating them and applying them to specific developments.

I found that if I gave certain muscles work to perform, similar to the eventual exercise I wanted them to do, I gained fine results. When speed development is the aim, the concentration should be on white muscle fibres because, in sprinting, they are required to work for a short period in a series of short, sharp contractions. Therefore, they require exercise which will allow for quick resistance pressures in a series of repetitions that are not too fatiguing but are sufficient to irritate all the fibres to react. I found that an isotonic exercise is best; the ground is not the movable object but the body is – and in springing up hills the athlete is performing an isotonic exercise similar to the movement needed in the eventual competition, but without the excess anaerobic strain.

Fundamentally, speed is developed in two ways – through longer strides and a faster stride frequency. To develop longer strides, you have to increase the power and flexibility of the legs; to increase stride frequency, you need to develop faster reflex action and better co-ordination, relaxation and technique as well as flexibility.

It is important, in all types of running, to have strong quadriceps to maintain good knee lift right through the distance you are running. Knee lift is relative to the speed at which you are running. A marathon runner will not run with a noticeably high knee action but he or she should be able to keep bringing the knees up much higher, not only because it stretches the stride but because it shortens the lever and gets the feet through high and fast for those seconds in which the runner wants the maximum output from his or her body.

Think about that lever: if you use a wrist action to move a three-metre-long rod, you will have no chance of moving its outer end as fast you could move the extremity of a ten-centimetre-long rod. The high knee lift has the same reaction with the movement of the foot because it shortens the lever effectively from hip-to-foot long to knee-to-foot long.

Failure to develop this quality far enough is evident in 400 metres running all round the world. I have watched far too many runners covering the last 50 metres with their knee lift gone, their upper bodies tightening and their legs beginning to waver because their quadriceps are not strong enough to maintain good knee lift. Most of them are good 300-metre runners. They merely stagger the last 50 to 100 metres up the home straight. If it can happen so easily and have such an effect over 400 metres, imagine what it can be like over longer distances.

So, head regularly for those steep hills and run up them to activate the big upper leg muscles. Make the muscles feel the exercise and keep at it steadily but do not try to run too fast. It is not designed to be an anaerobic development exercise.

Keep suppling and loosening exercises going on a regular basis during this stage, with particular attention to ankle flexibility. Too many runners, not realising what tremendous power is stored there, run with an inefficient ankle action. Watch the ankles of gymnasts and ballet dancers and you will see what great flexibility can be attained. The advantage to the runner because of increased striding efficiency is worth the little effort it takes to strengthen and flex ankles.

Throughout this speed build-up, watch your technique carefully. You must keep your running balanced and relaxed and maintain an economical stride length.

Now, back to determining your basic speed. You should be fit enough for the sprint that fixes it – run it over 200 metres rather than 100 metres because the way you start can affect the time too much over the shorter distance to give an accurate indication. Beyond 200 metres, stamina is required and this can also influence the result.

The sprint test is the best way to judge your potential. It is not your build or leg length or weight which influences your decision on the distance to aim for, it is your basic speed. If you cannot run 200 metres faster than 26 seconds, for instance, forget all about half-miling. All the training in the world will not make you an 800 metres champion.

HALBERG'S best 200 was about 24 seconds. To run 800 in 1:52, he was flat out all the way and near his best sprinting speed. He just could not run any faster. However, his stamina was such that, soon after running one 800 that fast, he could run another just as fast again; and he could extend running at or near the basic speed over distances twelve times as long - but in no way could he ever have become a great 800 metres runner.

The athlete who can run 22.5 for 200 is basically fast enough to become the Olympic 800 metres champion. SNELL proved that because he was a 22.3 man. George KERR could run 21 seconds, but he lacked the stamina to keep up the fast running all the way, whereas Snell was almost tireless at the distance. Roger MOENS, second to SNELL in the Rome 800 metres, and SNELL were the slowest 200 metres men in the field but both were stamina men and kept coming up fresh to run yet again at near their best basic speeds. Speedsters without stamina did not have a chance against them as long as the overall pace was kept on through the preliminaries and the final.

I have tested this theory and proved it so often that it really is not a theory any more. It is a fact you cannot go astray on, as you can if you try to judge a runner's potential on the way he or she looks. The average long-distance runner is the wiry type, the middle-distance runner is built more powerfully, along the lines of the top quarter-milers of the 1930s, and the sprinter is really powerful looking – but there are so many exceptions that presumptions on physical appearance are dangerous.

One well-known coach used physical yardsticks, like long slender feet, for choosing his best prospects. I often wonder how he would have classified the enormous hoofs at the ends of SNELL'S legs and how he would have assessed the difference between the 76 kg SNELL and the 57 kg HALBERG, milers of almost equal ability, but so unlike physically.

Athletes and coaches still fail to appreciate the significance and permanence of basic speed. As a result, a lot of runners are wasted by being put over distances they will never master, until running sours on them. One of New Zealand's first great half-milers, Doug HARRIS, plugged away for years as a run-of-the-mill sprinter. He switched to the half-mile because he was tired of being beaten and New Zealand found it had an international-class runner. He could have had a sub-four minute mile when others where still dreaming of it, but, unfortunately, he was spiked and forced out of the sport before he could gain the potential or the recognition he deserved.

This does not mean the sprinter would necessarily make a middle-distance champion; it does mean that many would-be sprint champions would make better middle-distance runners because they are beaten by their lack of basic speed before they even begin sprinting.

You can classify yourself further, into a puller or a driver. The puller is the runner who skims the grounds, without a great deal of apparent physical effort, and is usually ideal cross-country material. The driver works with a comparatively laboured style, and can get into trouble on rough or soft ground because he or she then has to drive harder to maintain speed and the exhaustion rate is accelerated.

Ireland's Ron DELANEY was a typical driver, hunched-up and visibly forcing himself; he did not look relaxed. HALBERG was a puller; he just drifted along.

The relaxation and economy of movement in the running of Barry MAGEE, who took the bronze medal in the Rome marathon, convinced me, long before he thought of racing the marathon, that he could become the greatest at the distance. He was the essence of conservation of effort and could run 65 kilometres without feeling tired. His endless glide was natural. I did not put it there. All I take credit for is recognising his potential and putting him at the distance for which he was best suited, and preparing the schedule that ran him to the top and would have kept him there if persistent leg trouble had not forced him to quit. Now, as a veteran, and with very little training, he can still run a 2:30 marathon.

Age also dictates your performance. You cannot be hurried into your best distance. For instance, a natural three-miler should be mature enough at 25 to produce his or her best running and should not be discouraged if still short of championship times at 22. It was this point that led me to predict HALBERG'S emergence as a world champion long before he did.

SNELL was a champion at 22 and had it within him to be the greatest runner in history. I still believe the quality of his running has not been bettered. When we wrote Run to the Top, I predicted a 3:47 mile, a 1:44 half-mile, a 13-minute three miles and a 27-minute six miles were all within reach of runners then in action. SNELL hit 1:44 only two years later with a remarkable solo run on a grass track.

SNELL, HALBERG and MAGEE all used their different basic speeds to best advantage and this is what is important in your running – to discover your basic speed so that you can begin setting targets with some prospect of achieving real success.

You are now at the stage of training when your maximum steady state should be as high as possible and you should be ready to accustom yourself to exercising anaerobically. Your schedule now incorporates small amounts of anaerobic running and this will progressively increase in intensity and volume.

This is, like most other phases, time consuming so you should now avoid unnecessary exercises. To develop speed, power, suppleness, technique and an increase in your anaerobic capacity gives you enough to concentrate on and any time wasted on anything else is improvement lost.

Running is, as I said before, the best exercise and, if you are a student or a worker, your time will be limited enough. So, because you may not have time to do all the necessary running and other essential activities separately, we have constructed running exercises which combine all the ingredients. Do them the right way and we not only save time but we achieve results just as if good as if we had used weights training to bring resistance to muscles for power development; calisthenics and gymnastics to improve suppleness, flexibility and speed; running training to upgrade technique; and further running to add to anaerobic capacity.

My schedules have been designed to combine all these aspects within each session. A caution here: the wise train only according to their age, physical condition and capacity to exercise. They learn quickly about themselves and train by that knowledge, increasing the volume and intensity of work only when they feel their condition can take it. If you try to train and race fast too soon, you are doomed to disappointment; you must understand clearly what you are attempting and what effects your exercising will have and you must work within that understanding.

Feel your way along patiently and do only what you feel capable of doing at each stage of each training session. The schedules in this book are only guides to what is the desirable optimum. They can be amended and the workload reduced and still produce excellent results, which is better than forcing yourself to training to the exact guideline limits.

Try to find a hill at least 300 metres long and rising at a gradient of about one in three on a road, in a park or a forest trail. The best layout is a circuit with a smallish, steep hill for uphill work, a less steep hill for downhill running and flattish areas both top and bottom for speed training and jogging.

When you begin training on your hill circuit, you run at warming-up pace for about two kilometres first. If temperatures permit, unnecessary clothing should be taken off to allow freedom of movement, which is most important in this phase of training.

At the base of the steeper hill, start springing up, on your toes, not running up, but bouncing. You have to lift and drop the body's centre of gravity to use your body weight as a form of resistance to the leg muscles. This gives you muscular development and flexibility through the leg's extreme actions, first in driving upwards with a high knee lift and then in taking the force of your body weight as it comes down. Drive hard, pushing upward with your toes, flexing your ankles as much as possible and, when you land on the forepart of your foot, let the heel come down below the level of the toes as the weight is taken. This stretches the calf muscles upwards and downwards as much as possible and applies resistance which thoroughly exercises muscle fibre.

As another example of the short lever principles I mentioned earlier, an ice skater spinning like a top on one spot can regulate turning speed by holding the arms out or keeping them close to the body. The turning speed slows when the arms are extended, quickens when the arms are drawn in to the body. So, if you want to develop fast strides or increase stride frequency, it follows that your feet will have to follow through as close to the buttocks as possible. If you move your feet through close to the ground, the stride is much slower. But you cannot bring your feet through with a high action unless you carry your hips forward. Some of the world's best sprinters run with, seemingly, a backward lean; while I do not suggest you exaggerate this action you must appreciate how it helps that comfortable, economical and fast leg action.

Concentrate on running with your head up and looking straight ahead. If you let your head fall forward, your hips tend to be held back and this does not allow the knee to rise high or the feet to follow through high.

I have watched athletes running with their hips back, a distinct forward lean and their heels kicking high at the back and they have always given me the feeling they are running into the ground. Their body attitude forces them to run with a short stride and prevents them from getting more speed out of themselves. I have seen athletes struggling to hold the field in a middle-distance race when, simply by shifting their hips forward a little, they could lengthen stride, probably with a reduction of the effort they are making, and maintain a much faster pace. This is not a question of conditioning or anything other than simply basic technique.

This is all part of the relaxed running mentioned earlier, a co-ordination of arm and legs, of relaxed arm, shoulder, neck and facial muscles.

So, with all this in mind, as you spring up that hill, your actions must be relaxed, with the head up and looking ahead, the hips slightly forward, the legs driving down forcefully, pushing hard with the toes, the knees rising high with a lifting of the centre of gravity and then the legs applying body weight resistance to the leg muscles as the feet hit the ground. Your progress up the hill will not be fast but gradual.

Do only as much hill-springing as your condition will allow and increase the workload only when your muscles become accustomed to it. At the top of the hill, take a recovery break by jogging easily on the flat. Do not stop running. Then, when you hit the downhill, you should run fast, striding relaxed but with a slightly longer stride length than normal. With no resistance against them, your muscles will be able to gain further recovery and there will be a general stretching which you feel in the legs, the stomach muscles and the hips. It will probably be a good reminder to do some exercises for your stomach muscles, to supple them for easier breathing when you are running under pressure and your heart and lungs have expanded. Unless the stomach muscles are supple, you will apply pressure to your diaphragm, pulling at the ligaments attaching the diaphragm to the skeleton, which is the cause of stomach cramps or stitch. If you have experienced stitch, you will know that it will slow your running dramatically and even stop you.

The downhill run tends to throw the body backwards, which stretches the stomach muscles and increases diaphragm pressure; it is a good exercise for bringing on an attack of stitch but it will, in time, help to condition you against it. You can help that improvement by doing sit-ups, with knees bent to avoid lower back strain, and backward bending exercises.

Be warned: if you are using a road for this training, it is imperative that you wear shoes with thick rubber soles and heels, not shoes with the heels cut away.

At the foot of the hill, use the flat section for sprint repetitions, varying them with each circuit you run. Use whatever distances you like from 50 metres to 400 metres but you should try, for best results, to use 50, 100, 200 and 400-metre windsprints. If the circuit is short, do the windsprints only every 15 minutes.

The reason for this is that we want to begin the development of your anaerobic exercise capacity. This is the beginning of the culmination of all the steady work you have been doing to lift your maximum steady state and you should adjust very quickly to anaerobic training – but you must keep its intensity to reasonable levels. It is not advisable to go suddenly into great volumes of intense anaerobic training, as many athletes do. Just as you have carefully built the aerobic steady state, so you must now raise carefully the capacity to exercise anaerobically without sacrificing any of the good condition you have established. That good condition is the foundation on which you build all your future strengths.

By confining the anaerobic work in these training sessions to the repetitions you can accomplish within a flat stretch of only 600 to 800 metres, you cannot possibly do too much. The benefit will accrue gradually but sufficiently without creating too much waste product.

Every stage of training is to be approached in the same gradual way to allow your body to accustom itself to the various new forms of exercise. You will rapidly feel the effects of the initial anaerobic work – a burning sensation in the throat and other immediate effects as you shift into speed work after the longer, slower road running and cross-country work you have been doing. You will also be sharply aware of the benefit week after week as your ability to handle the work becomes greater and the effort easier. Do it all thoroughly and sensibly and by the time you step out on the track you will be well-prepared to handle the stepped-up volume and greater intensity of the repetitions and interval work that will follow.

A mature runner in good condition should spend about an hour on the hill circuit session, plus fifteen minutes each for warming up and cooling down jogging. If you are a woman, a girl, a youth or a novice at this type of training, limit the work according to your capacity. The best value from the exercises comes from tackling them sensibly, not to excess. If your body insists it has had enough for the session and you have only been on the circuit half an hour, let it have its way.

If you have not got a hill to run on, do not despair. You can do the hill-springing work on flat ground because the resistance from the body weight will still be reasonably effective on the leg muscles, though the ankle flexing will not be as marked. You can supplement your training by standing on a raised object, such as a book or a block, on the balls of your feet and raising your heels up and down. You may be able to find a stadium or some other building with steps or stairs on which you can do the springing exercises – though the downhill striding would have to be equalled by doing relaxed fast striding on the flat with an exaggerated stride action.

The step running is actually one of the best exercises for improving speed. In Jacksonville, Florida, a few years ago I met a coach with a problem; where, in dead flat country like that around Jacksonville, do you do hill training? I pointed out a tall building about two miles away and suggested he would find his hill inside – the stairwell. A year or two later, that coach had trained his daughter to win her high school championship and his whole school team had been very successful. But the only change he made to his normal programme was to jog his team to the tall building, run them up the stairs to the eleventh floor, drop them back down in the elevator and run them up the stairs again before jogging them home. The early agony of the regime really paid off.

The uphill running can be varied. Instead of springing each time, try running up with a high knee lift to place most of the work on the quadriceps or front upper leg muscles, or concentrate the effort on the ankles, using them consciously to force the knees up. Then go back to hill-springing.

Hopping on one leg alternately is a useful exercise. So are frog hops: squat, hands on hips, and do a series of bounds in the squat position. Walking in the squat position helps upper leg muscles. If you want to add pressure to the frog hops, a small bag of sand on the shoulders does it without upsetting your balance.

Another exercise: bounding forward, driving hard off the back leg, with high knee lift and long strides and forcing the arms forward and up to help body momentum. It is a good exercise for co-ordination within the increased stride length.

The hill circuit programme lasts four to six weeks, depending on the runner's reactions and the time allowed in the overall schedule. During the period, you spend three days a week on a hill, alternating with three days of leg speed running and one of long running. I originally had my athletes spending more time on hill work but I found that, beyond six weeks, the effort of maintaining the pressure could cause dejection. This was particularly the case with the Venezuelans, who were either in high spirits or quite depressed, so with them I tried the alternation of hill work, leg speed work and long running and found I could still get the results, plus psychological changes which fully justified the change.

The regime can hurt the legs quite severely initially so watch your reactions and remember that it is better to underdo this phase than over-do it. Feel your way into a pattern that suits you. Only well-conditioned athletes will get through the full six weeks properly and successfully.

I should mention that in all the years I have trained athletes on this hill programme, I have not had one develop Achilles' tendon trouble, though it is an injury quite prevalent in sport today. Athletes are always running into tendon or hamstring trouble because they have not done their homework with supling and stretching exercises or hill work to build in the resistance as well as the extension of the important muscles and tendons.

Your mileage during this period will be about 150 kilometres a week, including warming-up and cooling down. Try to fit in other easy aerobic running each day to supplement this, because it helps recovery. Ideally, you should include about 30 minutes of supplementary running each day.

For the alternating leg speed training day, you need a flat area from 100 to 120 metres long and preferably with a slight gradual decline. Warm up for at least 15 minutes and then run over the course up to ten times, with about a three-minute jogging interval between each run – this is important because you must not rush this exercise – thinking only about moving your legs as fast as possible. Do not be conscious of stride length. Keep your upper body relaxed and the knee action reasonably high and think only of pulling the legs through as fast as you can by using the quadriceps and lower abdominal muscles.

The exercise is designed to overcome viscosity in the legs and to develop fine speed by making you pull your leg through fast rather than letting it swing through like a pendulum. Avoid running into the wind because you do not want any resistance.

It will also be helpful to do some relaxed striding over 100 metres with a 300 metres jogging interval up to ten times as a speed developer. Keep tall and upright; use high knee lift and drive hard off the back leg at a speed fast enough to be able to maintain balance. After the last repetition, cool down for at least 15 minutes by jogging easily.

This exercise will also give you tired legs but keep on with it and it will become progressively easier after about two weeks; by then, you will be getting excellent results.

So there it is: hill training three days a week; leg speed running and relaxed striding on the alternate days; and a long aerobic run on the seventh day – for from four to six weeks.

4   Track Training

Quite often I have watched runners training and then asked them what they were doing, what effect their training was having on their bodies, why they were doing what they were doing and what they believed they would achieve from it.

Mostly, they did not know. They were training blindly, guessing and hoping for good results. Some were slavishly following schedules that some champion or other had previously used but they did not understand the schedules or the general effects the programmes were having on them. Often, they never thought to ask their coaches why they were doing the particular work set for them. This is no way for athletes to train or to be trained; they must know why a certain exercise is being used and how it could and should affect them.

Even if you are well-conditioned, you can throw away your chances of success if you do not evaluate your exercises and get balance in your schedule. It is easy to make mistakes in track training and they can be disastrous; you could end up running your best times at unimportant meetings and coming up to the big ones off-peak; or levelling off your performance too soon; or never getting to your potential at all.

Many coaches and athletes incline to overvalue track training and the worth of track schedules, not realising that the most important training is the conditioning of the body to prepare it for anaerobic training and racing. Without that preparation, track schedules are not worth the paper on which they are written.

I say the same about the track schedules in this book. They are a guide for coaches and athletes preparing their own – but if you do not condition first, they are worthless. No cake is successful if the vital ingredients are left out.

When you move into track training, you must evaluate all the types of running training available; you must balance your schedule to get the best possible results from the conditioning work you have already done. The tempo of training must be increased gradually and your speed carefully controlled if you want to achieve the ultimate racing form on the day or days you most want it. Patience, as in all phases of training, is imperative.

You will need increased volumes and intensities of anaerobic training, you will need sprint training, fast relaxed running and sprint racing to develop speed; you will need sharpening training to bring you to racing form; you will need time trials to co-ordinate stamina and speed; you will need racing in sprint, middle and distance races to improve racing condition and experience and for further co-ordinating.

Your original plan was to develop enough stamina to maintain the necessary speed over the distance of the race you are training for. By now, you should have that endurance; now, you are ready to absorb the speed. It should be quite clear to you by now that your speed has not developed fully. This is one of the areas where patience can be strained. Many runners have difficulty in seeing beyond what they are doing at the moment and, if what they are doing seems to be producing minimal results, they either begin forcing themselves or lose interest. If you can accept that the slow progression is the only way, you will not have this problem.

Speed has not been of particular importance in your training so far. Now it becomes of prime importance. It is the target of the next phase of training, with its more intense anaerobic activity.

Another warning: many athletes make the mistake of running in hard races before they fully develop their speed. They find themselves unable to foot it with the rest, though they finish feeling as if they could run the race all over again, and this inability to produce speed in their running is a frustration.

Intense training sessions of anaerobic repetitions will not necessarily develop that speed, because the volume of work involved and the increase in lactic acid formed preclude the possibility of top speeds being used. But the workouts will develop further your capacity to exercise anaerobically.

One of the best ways is to use the typical training of fast relaxed speed running over distances from 100 to 150 metres, with recovery intervals of at least three minutes between each run so you can develop your same top speed again and again.

The fundamentals of building speed have to be watched carefully. The sprint training workout should incorporate three elements in particular recommended by Bud WINTER – some high knee exercise running, some ankle-flex and driving running and some running tall – in conjunction with the fast relaxed speed running.

A typical workout, depending on your age and other factors, would be: a proper warm-up; some suppling and loosening exercises; a run over 80 to 100 metres with shoulders and arms relaxed, on the toes, pulling the knees up high and using a fast leg action with slow forward momentum; a three-minute jog or walk; then run through it again – always working with the wind behind you so that there is no natural resistance.

Go through again, this time bringing the knees well up but driving hard forward so that the ankles, being accustomed to the maximum flexing from hill work, are flexed hard like a spring to force you forward. The arms should be forced forward to help you lift to the longer stride length. The exercise should be done twice, with a three-minute recovery interval.

Then, also twice, run down the track high on your toes, with good knee lift, concentrating on lifting your body from the pelvis. Percy CERUTTY and Bud WINTER both recommended this and it is a good method for making the utmost of stride length and putting spring into the stride and body lift into your running action.

Then run twice over the course but faster, running tall but concentrating on all three aspects – stride length, spring and body lift. All three should be kept in mind in the following fast running.

Using the straight of the track that has the following wind, if any, stride fast and relaxed the length of the straight and then jog easily round the rest of the circuit. Repeat up to six or eight times according to your development and fitness. Then cool down by jogging for about 15 minutes or more.

This initial track training should not be at full speed, except for the sprint training. It is better to hold the tempo back a little so that it can be raised as you progress. Speed should always be held in check or you will lose control of racing form later.

When your schedule is arranged and the various runs timed, pay attention to your capabilities and present condition. Do not hesitate to allow reasonable timing for each training run. Later on, you should try to run to previously determined times but not faster. As always, you must have a clear picture in your mind of what you are doing, why you are doing it and what the short-term and long-term effects are going to be.

Training should never be raced. This is a mistake many runners make. They sharpen to racing condition before they reach the best co-ordination of stamina and speed and they do not get the best possible results. It is not easy for the well-conditioned runner to stop, or be stopped by his or her coach, from seeing during early training sessions how fast they can run – but you should not and you must not. I have known coaches, eager to see what their charges can do, run the fine edge right off them.

If careful speed control is maintained, ten weeks of track training before the important competition for which you are training should not be found too long. A well-conditioned runner will show good results on less than this but the best results are possible if more time is taken, with a slower rise in tempo and rigid exercise of speed control.

Schedules in this book have been used successfully in various international competitions and to break world records so they are a reasonable guide. But they are only a guide. Do not stick strictly to them simply because you feel you have to. All athletes are different, with individual strengths and weaknesses and these are aspects which you need to consider carefully in shaping the schedules to suit you.

You need knowledge of exercise evaluation if you want to use the most suitable daily exercises for the ultimate co-ordinated effort. So study them carefully as they appear in the schedules. For example:

Fartlek – Swedish for speed play, this involves running at various speeds over forest trails, parks and country at will. It is invaluable throughout training because of the environmental effects, which allow for subconscious control of efforts. It incorporates aerobic and anaerobic running, usually according to the condition and capabilities of the runner on the day. Stride out here, sprint there, jog somewhere else, spring up a hill and so on. Easy fartlek is ideal for helping recovery from hard training and racing. Hard fartlek can be used to develop the anaerobic capacity to exercise.

Paarlauf – This can be used for anaerobic capacity development, speed development and sharpening, depending on the number of runners taking part, the distances run and the length of each session. It has value because it is training with a competitive touch and the athlete often uses extra effort subconsciously. It is a form of relay racing, using predetermined distances round the track with an overlap of one runner. Runners continue to race other teams until stopped by a signal at a pre-determined time, say four minutes.

Time trials – Give your body a certain exercise to do often enough and it becomes efficient at it. The same is true of running over certain distances. The idea is to run trials under or at the distance being trained for – 600 and 700 metres trials for the 800; or 1,000 and 1,200 metres trials for the 1,500; but the actual race distances for 3,000 and 5,000 metres runners; and 5,000 metres with an occasional 10,000 for 10,000 metres runners. The under-distance trials for the shorter distances are best because of the high speeds used and the resulting oxygen debts.

Steeplechasers should run their trials over the actual distance but on most occasions it would be wise to change the water jump for another hurdle.

The effort used should be near to racing effort without increasing the speed over the final stage. Strong, even running is the correct approach. Time trials co-ordinate speed and stamina and find out weaknesses and strengths which indicate any adjustments that need to be made to training, what racing is needed to improve the weaknesses and to capitalise on the strengths.

Starting practice – For middle-distance runners, this exercise helps by improving reflexes and sharpening and co-ordinating body actions, particularly when the starting command intervals are varied. The starts can be run out over 30, 40 and 50 metres.

Repetitions – These are usually used for the development of the anaerobic capacity by varying the numbers run, the distance run, the times that each run takes and the interval taken. It is called interval training when control of the interval is considered important but it is optional whether you use this training – and do it as you feel like it rather than to fixed requirements – or select other anaerobic training.

In the repetitions system, you run until the oxygen debt incurred makes you feel tired, indicating that you have lowered your blood pH level. The times of the repetitions and the intervals, the number of the repetitions and the distances run are not really important. If you have lowered your pH level at the end of the session, you have achieved what you set out to do. You are usually the best judge of when you have had enough.

The repetition numbers given in the schedules, therefore, are only a guide to what you could expect to do or aim for. They are not to be taken as imperatives.

Sharpeners – These are introduced at a stage when it is still necessary to do some anaerobic training but advisable to drop the volume and increase the intensity. If you run 20 x 400 metres, you will be at it a long time and you will become very tired; but if you run five laps of the track by sprinting 50 metres in every 100 metres, floating the other 50, to give you 20 sharp sprints in all, you will be extremely tired in the running muscles, but will have taken only seven minutes or so. Sharpening puts the knife edge on anaerobic training capacity without pulling down the good condition you have carefully built up. It is best to use sharpeners only once a week, early during the training schedule week.

Sprint training – Purely for the development of speed. Technique training with concentration on an upright body carriage, keeping up tall, a relaxed upper body, good knee lift, leg drive and use of the ankles. Allow good recovery intervals between fast runs.

The first four weeks of track training should comprise anaerobic capacity development training to get this level as high as possible, as well as concentration on speed work to improve sprinting ability to near maximum. This training should be alternated day by day to allow for recovery from the harder anaerobic running. If you feel that recovery from anaerobic training two days previously is not sufficient, it is unwise to do more. You must let the pH level recover to near normal before you pull it down again. You should supplement this training as much as possible. You should allow at least 15 minutes for warming-up and cooling down jogging and add supplementary jogging at any time of the day available to you.

When I was training my team in the Owairaka area of Auckland, we would run four miles (6 $\frac{1}{2}$ kilometres) to the track at New Lynn rather than use the local one because it gave us an extra eight miles (13 kilometres) of easy training running each day to supplement the scheduled workload.

At the Mexico Olympics, I talked to the West German rowing coach about why his team had not been successful in previous years and why, this time, they had succeeded. He told me that, previously, they had loaded their boats on a vehicle and had all driven to the lake for training and then driven back again. This time, they put the boats on the canal and rowed the six kilometres to and from the lake. A lot of people did not believe this was the only change he had made but it made the same kind of sense that I am offering now.

The supplementary work helps recovery from anaerobic training and keeps the oxygen uptake level high. This is a period of exacting, tiring training during which it is advisable not to try to race because it will be impossible for you to return good performances. Just concentrate on developing anaerobic capacity and speed – two or three days of anaerobic training, two or three of speed or sprint training and the balance in jogging, easy striding for technique, or easy fartlek. It is up to you to decide what to do day by day in light of your reactions to previous training. Protect your good condition and let the training tempo build up gradually.

Track training should continue for about 4 $\frac{1}{2}$ weeks. With your anaerobic capacity to exercise, your speed and your stamina by then more or less developed and co-ordinated, you now have to aim to run smoothly through your competitions without apparent weaknesses in your running. You might have fine speed, stamina and anaerobic capacity, but this does not necessarily mean you can race to your best potential. This is why time trials and development racing are now needed. We call them development races because you are still training quite hard and you cannot continue that and expect to run your best races at the same time. This is the mistake made by runners the world over.

Use sharpeners at least once a week to maintain the anaerobic level. Pay attention to the maintenance of speed as well; you should run at least one sprint race a week on the same day as the mid-week or less important competition or time trial training session. One day should be used for a longish aerobic run to help recovery; easy fartlek running can also help. Easy striding and jogging on the days before the hardest race of the week will be beneficial.

A schedule for this period could be: Monday, sharpeners; Tuesday, sprint training or easy fartlek; Wednesday, time trial or more sprints and middle distance; Thursday, use for co-ordinating, according to the results of the time trials or racing (say, pace-judgement runs, fartlek, more sharpeners, sprint training or striding); Friday, jogging or easy fartlek; Saturday, race over or near your racing distance or time trial; Sunday, a long, easy, aerobic run.

The last time trial should be run about ten days before the first important competition you are training for and it should be run at your best effort.

During the last 1 $\frac{1}{2}$ weeks before that important race, you should try to freshen up by lightening the training to build your mental and physical reserves. Some have named this period 'overcompensation' and it is important; so you should test the period of time you need individually through trial and error methods in less important competitions. People differ in the times they need, though the ten days seems to suit most. You should train every day during this period but well within your capabilities. Any fast running should be short and intense, not prolonged, and the longer runs should be made at easy effort.

Watch your food intake during this period. There is a tendency when you ease up in training to overeat. It is not desirable to put on any weight and if you are susceptible to easy weight gain, take particular care.

When you reach the main competitions, it is important to realise that you are now trained to race and not to train hard any longer. Again, this is a mistake many athletes make. You need only to keep sharp and fresh to race really well again and again and you cannot do this if you try to train hard. A typical week's schedule for this period can be: Saturday, race; Sunday, an easy, longish run; Monday, a few sharpeners or easy fartlek; Tuesday, light sprint training or stride-outs; Wednesday, sprint and middle distance or underdistance races; Thursday, jog; Friday, stride-outs, etc. If you do not race twice a week, replace those races with time trials.

Always be guided day to day in your training by your reactions to the previous day's exercise. Every day, do some supplementary long aerobic running, either in morning jogs or in good cooling down runs after racing or training. This helps to maintain your good condition. Pay attention to your legs the day after fast training or racing; if they feel dead, with no bounce, do not do anaerobic training in any volume. It is wise to go for an easy jog.

During the latter stages of track training, it is not possible to be too specific because different runners have different strengths and weaknesses and will react differently to the co-ordinating training. So it is important to analyse carefully the training results of development races and time trials and aim your subsequent training and repairing any weaknesses that seem apparent. As long as the daily exercises are evaluated and you learn from any mistakes you might make, and are confident that you are doing the training you need, you should gain a fine balance and the desired results. Always be intelligent and systematic.

5   Cross-country Training and Racing

Cross-country running is of great benefit to track runners and other athletes as a general conditioner. The ground you run over is usually uneven and undulating and subjects leg muscles and tendons to various resistances you do not encounter on even surfaces. This adds suppleness and strength. On soft ground, your heels and toes sink deeper, which gives the ankles greater range of movement and eventually improves flexibility.

Athletes who run with stiff or taut upper body muscles or use an exaggerated leg driving action can develop more relaxed and economical running techniques by training and racing cross-country. We have already explained that relaxed running is vital in reaching optimum results.

If you feel you are not as relaxed as you would like to be, get out on muddy, sandy or soft ground where it is difficult to gain a good footing and traction is low. You will soon learn that driving hard on these surfaces consumes energy fast and is extremely tiring. You will also learn that the best solution is to relax the upper body muscles, keep the arm action low, hold the hips forward and develop a pulling action rather than a driving one. The effort of forward movement will then be reduced to a minimum.

Poorly conditioned runners tend to run with tight upper body muscles and high arm carriage and the more tired they get the worse these faults become and the more uneconomic their running is. Working on country that forces you to relax and economise to handle it effectively makes good sense.

The hilly terrains of cross-country courses have another value. Hill running adds resistance and provides a further dimension in the encouragement of ankle flexibility. Running uphill develops power and ankle suppleness which emerges later in a more driving natural stride. The steeper the hills the more the ankle and leg muscles will have to flex.

The heavy runner will find this uphill running much more difficult but the resistance to the leg muscles will add speed, power and muscular endurance no matter what shape and weight you are or how much you are forced to struggle. The greater the body weight, the more energy is needed to lift the body against gravity.

Running up hills forces the knees to lift higher, one of the most desirable developments for any runner, because this governs stride speed and length. It also develops the muscle fibres, increasing power. Both red and white fibres improve in efficiency through hill training.

The lightweight can usually beat the heavyweight over hilly cross-country and track steeplechase courses but this should not discourage the heavily-built athlete. Everyone can gain vastly from cross-country work. I have found invariably that the runners who do not like cross-country work are those who need it most and find it most difficult to handle. The cause of their dislike is usually poor and uneconomical technique. These are the ones who have to persevere to overcome their faults and the place to do it is on cross-country.

Downhill striding on soft ground is another good exercise. It helps to loosen you up around the hips, relax, stretch out muscles and tendons which you would not do on hard downhill runs because of the jarring. I think it could also help to a degree in building leg speed.

Training over country, on forest trails or around golf courses or parks has a psychological value, too. The pressure is off and you will find yourself responding to the inviting contours of the land, speeding up and down according to the conditions and your reactions to the exercise. Since accurate timing is not possible, you tend to settle down to running at speeds that tire you pleasantly, rather than exhaust you. This pace is often near your best aerobic speed but you achieve it in a relaxed frame of mind. Runners seldom train over country at sustained anaerobic speeds unless they are carrying out some form of hard fartlek – and that is a type of training only used in the more advanced stages of physical fitness.

Racing cross-country is also psychologically good for you. These races lack the nervous tensions of track and road races because you are mostly away from the critical eyes and urgings of the spectators. The speed running is not sustained so the overload tends to be placed on the muscular system and eases the pressure on the cardiac system. This reduces the oxygen debt and allows for reasonable states of fatigue, rather than excessive ones. There is no question that the presence of spectators influences tired runners to strive to maintain uneconomic speeds; over country, your audience loses sight of you and there is no feeling of loss of face if you slow your speed to counter tiredness. Your running is generally much more relaxed.

Despite this, cross-country is a good disciplinarian. You will subconsciously control your effort to be more economical and this is probably its greatest asset as an initial general conditioning exercise. Later, it becomes important for runners to maintain controlled pressure on themselves over measured courses to ensure further development but, initially, this is not needed and cross-country running helps you to avoid it.

The times run during cross-country racing and training should not be treated with too much importance. Courses and weather and ground conditions vary so much from day to day and have such an effect on performance that to try to chart progressive times can only be confusing and misleading. The aim is to keep to an estimated effort schedule.

Cross-country will emphasise the value of calisthenics and suppling and stretching exercises. They help in handling fences, hurdles and other obstacles encountered during racing and training. In fact, you should practise hurdling and clearing fences regularly for confidence and efficiency. The first time you come to them, fences and hurdles can look pretty daunting and can cost you time; with practice, they become more of an interesting challenge to your technique. You need to learn one and two-handed vaults, clear jumps, hurdling and even rolling underneath them.

Before you race over a course which is strange to you, try to jog or walk it, try clearing the various obstacles and practise on them until you feel confident and have worked out the best approaches to make. Knowing always what is ahead of you is a big advantage in cross-country.

If you intend to train seriously for cross-country events, as well as using it for its conditioning value, you should work to a schedule for about ten weeks before the particular race you are aiming for. This schedule, outlined later, is a mixture of anaerobic running, including sharpeners and longer repetitions, time trials and races over and near to the distance you are training for. Before you enter this schedule, you need two or three months of aerobic cross-country running, especially if you have been competing on the track. If you are in poor condition, the aerobic conditioning period needs to be longer.

In some countries, cross-country courses are nothing better than glorified track races, particularly in many American states, which run cross-country on flat lawn-like areas. This is not cross-country; it lets you run almost as you would on the road, with fast, sustained speed running, which really does not help to develop condition because the exercise becomes sustained and anaerobic, and encourages cardiac fatigue. Many of the courses do not even have obstacles.

Athletes who compete on this type of course once or twice a week for ten weeks will invariably pull their condition down. It is the tough, rugged courses with everything underfoot from hard ground to swamps that give you the benefits you need.

Back in 1950, when I left the Lynndale club in Auckland and joined Owairaka, I was faced with an interesting challenge. Lynndale then was the strongest cross-country club in New Zealand and Owairaka was barely developed – I began with only six runners. But in four years, Owairaka was the top club in the country.

A principal reason then was that the young people in the Owairaka area, though they just came along to run, were trained and developed on one of the most rugged cross-country courses you will find anywhere. HALBERG, SNELL, Jeff JULIAN, MAGEE and all my other runners were trained extensively on this course.

So, whether you are an athlete or coach, consider these facts about cross-country as an important facet of preparation for track racing: you need good obstacles, hills, muddy ground and some flat fast running – a real mixture that tests runners in several ways and slows them down through muscular fatigue as they hit the resistance of the hills but allows them to speed up on the flat sections. The runner will gain suppleness from training for obstacles and learn to relax by jumping small streams and bogs and covering soft ground. It is a great developer for sprinters, middle and distance runners and it would probably help athletes to condition for a number of other sports as well.

Track athletes should regard the cross-country season as a chance to build up general condition, to race as often as advisable, always concentrating on a relaxed running action and getting to enjoy the environment in which they are exercising. Whether it is woods, parkland or rough pasture, it will make a surprising contribution to your development, physically, mentally and technically.

6   Warming-up, Cooling down

An American coach from Abilene College told me he flew to Sacramento some years ago to hear a lecture by the Australian who coached Herb ELLIOTT, PERCY CERUTTY. In the question and answer period, PERCY was asked what he thought about warming-up. What do you want to warm up for, PERCY replied, rabbits do not and they can run like the very devil. Knowing PERCY as I did, I realise he was only saying this to make people think, but the Abilene coach and others took him seriously. He was then regarded as the greatest coach in the world.

The Abilene coach said he could not get home fast enough to find out if what PERCY said about rabbits was true. He knew where he could find a warren and he was out there before daybreak with a movie camera. He finally filmed a rabbit that came out from its burrow, sat on its hind legs, looked around and trotted back and forth several times before suddenly sharpening up and taking off across the field. So, said the Abilene coach, rabbits DO warm up and I have got a film to prove it. PERCY had made him think, and question and find the answers for himself.

Watch runners warming up for middle and distance races and you will notice a big difference in the times they take. Various factors influence athletes to have different warm-ups but the important thing to understand first is why you need to warm up at all.

One main reason is to raise the blood circulation to a pulse rate of somewhere near 130 to 140 beats a minute so that you do not have to go through the gears in your race; a second is to raise the body temperature and warm the muscles so they function more efficiently. This reduces the risk of pulling a muscle or straining a tendon. Warming-up overcomes muscle viscosity and sets you free to run easily at your best effort.

Years ago, athletes did not bother with the warm-up, planning early in a middle or distance race to get what was known as 'the second wind'. This is what you now achieve by warming-up properly; it is obvious commonsense to get through this difficult and possibly risky period before you begin racing rather than when you are under the strain of running competitively and unable to control your effort without risking your position in the field. When a muscle is cold, it is tight and less efficient. Warmth brings softness, reduces viscosity and allows for faster contraction.

Some athletes also perform stretching exercises in the warm-up but what you do and how you do it depends on the type of competition you are in. The steeplechase, for instance, calls for some calisthenics to prepare you for the hurdles. But it is a matter of preference; some runners ignore calisthenics and confine their activity to running at various speeds; others who regularly use calisthenics in their training usually include them in the warm-up. As long as you understand what you are trying to achieve and use the exercises that achieve this goal, it is not too important.

Time your warm-up according to the conditions of the day. If it is windy and cold, it is going to take you longer to get warm, even if you wear more and warmer clothing, but do not forget that, hot or cold, your pulse rate will begin rising as soon as you start running.

Many athletes warm up too long. Some run for 30 to 45 minutes or even longer on a day with a moderate temperature and reasonably good conditions; they could lift their pulse rates and body temperatures to the required levels in 15 minutes or even less. They get involved in long warm-ups because mostly they do not really understand the way of it.

In 1968, I arrived at the venue of the Finnish marathon championship about an hour before the start and saw some of the runners already warming up. They certainly did not understand what they were doing because some were running possibly faster than they would be halfway through the race. And that is the way it turned out for them; a marathon does not really need to be warmed up for with any serious activity. As long as the pulse rate and body temperature are elevated above normal, the marathon runner will be fine because the initial pace is never as fast as it is in a track race. Those who do go off like CERUTTY'S startled rabbits invariably drop back after a few kilometres.

Fifteen minutes is long enough for middle and distance racing. You should begin with seven or eight minutes at a good aerobic speed, follow with some 50 to 100-metre wind sprints according to how you feel – about three is usually enough – and then jog easily to hold the pulse and body warmth up. Just before the race, discard your tracksuit but keep moving about easily until you are called to the mark.

Do not make the mistake some runners do: They warm up adequately and then lie down under a blanket for five or more minutes. They stay warm but they let their pulse rates fall, which wipes out the point of the warm-up.

The runner who warms up for long periods gains nothing more physiologically than the one who confines himself or herself to 15 minutes, unless he or she is a nervous type who is more at ease trotting around than sitting thinking about the race and adding to the tension. Psychologically, as well, it might be better for that runner to keep moving; if he or she has a solid background of endurance running training it will not do any harm, except perhaps before a marathon or cross-country when it is essential to conserve all the energy possible.

Cooling down, or warming down, is equally important after you finish your race. During the run, your pulse rate is high, with blood gushing through the circulatory and respiratory systems under great pressure from the heart. When you stop and the pressure from the heart diminishes, many of the lesser arteries, arterioles, capillary beds and veins begin to contract, stemming the flow of blood. This can result in some blood of an acid nature, caused by the lactic acid created during the race, remaining in the muscles.

It is advisable to remove this blood from the muscle areas and replace it with blood of a higher pH; and the best way to do this is by stimulating the circulation of the blood in a way that will not create further oxygen debts. Continuing to jog easily for up to 15 minutes or so after the race will do this. Lactic acid does not leave the body but is converted to glycogen through chemical processes within the body's metabolism. The warm-down also allows body temperature to return to normal slowly and lessens the possibility of chills.

Think about your cool-down seriously. A lot of runners fail to recognise its value and they can suffer from sore leg muscles, caused by the acidic blood staying in the muscles and irritating muscle nerves. You can try to circulate the acidic blood away with massage but it is far better to let the heart do it for you while you jog quietly. You get the added benefit of breathing in large quantities of oxygen while you are jogging.

In 1957, the Finn SALSOLA broke the world 1,500 metres record in unusual circumstances. He normally had a warm-up of 45 to 50 minutes but this day he was resting in his hotel near the track in Turku and the person who was supposed to call him forget to do so. SALSOLA was not missed until the field was called together seven minutes before the start. In a mad flurry, he was contacted and rushed to the track. He had been lying on his bed and was quite warm but he had not time for his customary long warm-up and after only a few wind sprints was on the starting line. He won the race in world record time. His reaction was: *"What would I have done with a proper warm-up?"*

The answer to that is that he never again ran that fast, despite his long warm-ups.

7   Clothing and Shoes for Training and Racing

The clothing you wear will be governed by the conditions in which you have to train and race. In warmer climates, you do not need tracksuits for conditioning training or for much of the track training but you will need a waterproof windbreaker with a zip up the front to keep you dry and warm in heavy rain. The zip can be used to control the temperature in the windbreaker.

If you can, it is better and easier to train with very light clothing and not be hampered by a tracksuit which can overheat you and, in wet weather, can be too heavy. In cold climates, however, a tracksuit is a necessity for winter training. The weight of the suit will be determined by the severity of the cold.

In temperatures below minus 20°C, it pays to wear two tracksuits, as we did in Finland – one of material which allows air to pass through, worn under one of material which will not let the air through. This keeps the cold air out and creates a cushion of warm air between the outer suit and your body. With this outfit, you can run in 40°C below for two hours or more without trouble.

Shoes are possibly the most important item of equipment, so take your time when you are buying them. Try both shoes on; stand up and walk in them, feeling for any pressure points that could cause you problems. They should not bite into the heels at the Achilles' tendon; they should not be too tight across the joints of your feet; and they should not touch the ends of your toes, because once you begin running your feet can swell and move a little and you could lose your toe-nails. Your toes should be just clear of the end of the shoes because if the shoe is too long the joint of the foot, where the forepart is widest, will come back into the narrower waist of the shoe and you will suffer blistering on the inside of the foot.

Check that the shoes have good rubber soles that will protect you from the impact of hard training surfaces. If the heels have been cut away, they will be no good for road training because you need that rubber on the back edge of the heels to take the jarring when you run downhill. It is a vital part of a road-training shoe. Some manufacturers slope the back of the heels because it causes less wear but it does not protect the runner.

Some shoes are oversprung. By this I mean that when the shoe is taken off the last it will spring flat on the toe instead of staying like a box. This means the upper will pull down on the toe-nails and you will almost certainly lose them. You will not be able to fit the toes as near the front of the shoe as you should either, so you will lose traction trying to push off your toes with half an inch of empty shoe in the way.

Many running shoes are made on a straight last – but have a good look at your foot. It is more of a banana shape, with a slight curve. When you fit that into a straight shoe, you will get pressure on the outside of the big toe and your heel will try to get over the inside of the shoe heel and cause another pressure point.

To control this fault, some shoe makers insert a hard stiffener or counter, which then forces the forepart of the foot to overhang the edge of the sole on the outside of the shoe. Since, when you run, your foot tends to want to go outside anyway, you will find it going right over and causing ankle problems. Plus, probably, the rapid collapse of the shoe.

The straight shoe-banana foot mix is the main reason many runners need orthotics in their shoes, trying to get balance in unbalanced footwear.

The rubber soles and heels need to be semi-resilient. Drop hard rubber and it will not bounce. Drop soft rubber and it will not bounce. Drop rubber of the correct texture, a semi-microcellular formation, and it will bounce. This is important for anyone running a big mileage. Check this carefully; the mere fact that a shoe seems to have a lot of rubber under it does not mean you will get a lot of protection. It must be the right rubber.

The waffle sole is ideal for running on trails or grassy areas but on the road it wears down quickly and it robs you of traction. The more sole you can plant on the road, the better. The dragster driver uses the widest, flattest tyres available. Runners should, too. The traction loss with waffle soles on wet roads is particularly bad.

Peter SNELL was a comparative novice when he went to the Rome Olympics in 1960. He had learnt to run on grass tracks because New Zealand then had no hard tracks so we were unaware we faced a particular problem. Cinder and other hard surface tracks can be severe on middle-distance runners who run heel and toe until they sprint. SNELL, unused to hard tracks, was scheduled to run four tough races in three days which we knew could knock his legs around and cause severe muscle tightness and soreness.

So I made him a special pair of spikes and added a small rubber lift on the heels. When he reached the finals, we found that Adidas had persuaded the rest of the finalists to wear their shoes but, fortunately, they must have decided Peter had no chance at all because they did not bother to approach him. So he climbed on the winner's dais wearing his plain white spikes, which was not the effect Adidas had in mind.

However, they were curious about their construction so we told them the heel had been padded to avoid damage to the red cells in the blood, which would gather in the arterioles and capillaries and cause progressive breakdown in the legs. Out of that experience, Adidas produced what became known as the interval shoe, with a special rubber heel.

A point to remember about rubber is that, being temperature sensitive, it will harden in cold weather, reducing traction and cushioning against jarring. A greater degree of softness in the rubber is advisable to counter that condition.

For cross-country running, spiked shoes more solidly and strongly built than track shoes are needed to get you over muddy terrain and rough ground. Those conditions wreck track shoes. Orienteering runners use shoes with rubber-studded soles which grip well on slippery soles and are designed for hard wear.

The interval type of track shoe with the rubber heel wedge to absorb jarring is best for middle and distance running on the track.

Look for track shoes that have a good placement of screw-in spikes. The spikes should be as near to the toe as possible because this is where you get your forward drive and you are looking for maximum traction. The spikes should be under the outer edge of the forepart of the shoe – your feet will roll on to the outside of the joints, particularly when you are rounding the bends.

Lacing is far more important than runners realise. They should be threaded so that when they are tightened they do not pull down on the sinews and metatarsals on the top of the foot. A simple matter like lacing can prevent the foot from functioning freely and, because it may be straining against restrictive points, the foot can be damaged. We have included a lacing diagram to show how it is done to use the shoe itself to protect you from lacing pressure.

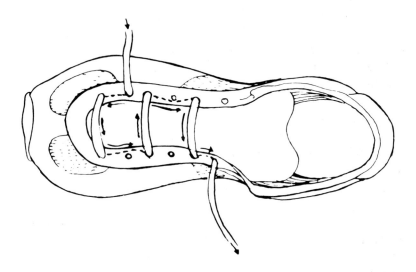

Watch heel wear on your shoes closely. Excessive wear leads to stress right through the leg and hip and can also cause bone wear.

Your running shorts should fit comfortably and not drag on your legs when your knees come up. If they do, you can expect problems on wet days when the drag is accentuated. For men, athletic supports seem to be a thing of the past; they can cause chafing. It is much better, if you do not have shorts with a sewn-in support, to use women's cotton briefs.

I was in a training camp in Woodville, north-east Texas, in 1970 when about 30 of us went for a 22-mile (34-kilometre) run on a hot and humid day. The American boys wore broad smiles of amusement when they saw me changing into cotton briefs which were obviously designed for a woman; but at the end of the run I was the only one not complaining of chafing. The next day, about 30 runners trooped into the local drapery and asked the woman behind the counter to fit them out in women's briefs. She looked rather alarmed until it was explained to her why so many men wanted feminine underwear. She did great business.

Running without some kind of support under your running shorts is cool and comfortable – but the continual strain imposed could cause problems.

Hooded and warm top shirts are useful for training in cold dry weather and for warming-up on cold days.

If you are a middle or distance runner, do not buy a stopwatch which does not have a full 60-second dial. The 30-second sweeps can cause confusion, particularly if you are trying to time more than one runner in trials or races or if you are trying to get an accurate reading while you are running. Some watches have a splits hand which can be stopped and started again without stopping the main timing hand: this is invaluable for accurate lap and other split times.

Stopwatches are expensive and it pays to think before you choose the one that is most suitable for your purpose. The digital types now available leave no doubts about the actual time elapsed and are an improvement on the standard type. One particular advantage is that the conventional stopwatch is usually slowed down if you carry it while you are running; the digital type is not affected.

8 Tactics

Middle and distance running is governed by eleven elements, all of which can be considered as tactical:

1. The athlete's basic abilities and development
2. Basic speed or the ability to sprint
3. Endurance
4. Ability to maintain a fast steady pace
5. Ability to vary speed in a race
6. The most suitable distance for a finishing kick
7. Ability to exercise control during a race
8. Consideration of opposing runners' abilities
9. Ability to observe, assess and exploit any strengths and weaknesses in the opposition
10. Ability to relate one's own weaknesses and strengths to the opposition
11. Ability to judge pace.

You must always be realistic and understand your limitations in running certain distances and, within that context, consider all the above principles – particularly that of basic speed.

Some runners are at a disadvantage because they do not have good basic speed and must, of necessity, try to force the pace in most of their races. They fear the final fast kick of their opponents and have to work hard to try to take that kick out of them. Very often, this can be achieved; but there are exceptions.

For instance, if the wind is strong, the fast runners can sit on the one forcing the pace, letting the wind take its toll of him or her and setting up the situation for a sprint finish when the leader is tired out. In such conditions, it is usually unwise for the staying type to make too much use of himself or herself by setting the pace too much. It is better to pin everything on a prolonged sprint from, say, 500 metres or so, which would stretch the opposition's stamina and possibly weaken them for the final sprint up the straight. If you are trying this tactic, however, beware that you do not run out of energy yourself.

It would pay you to try yourself out over various distances to be sure of the most suitable distance from the finish from which to begin your finishing run. Some runners can pick up speed quickly; others have to build to a sprinting speed gradually. If you can kick fast, it is all right to be near to or in front when you kick; if you cannot, you would be wise to stay back a few metres to give yourself the distance in which to wind up fully before you go past the leaders. Otherwise, you will find that you will merely take them with you and you will not have gained any advantage from being the one who broke first.

This is very much a situation in which you need to know your opposition; anyone in that field, behind you or in front, could produce a faster kick and get the drop on you before you have built up your own sprint. Again, trial and error methods should show you the most suitable kicking distance for your ability.

Runners with questionable stamina have been known to try to slow the pace by taking the lead and gradually easing their speed down. This can work at times but, in most races, other runners soon realise what is happening and go round the leader to put the speed back on. Then, the runner trying to ease the pace must try again to lead. Invariably, this leads to a series of sprints and spurts which take most toll of the runner who lacks the stamina and reduces his or her chances rather than enhancing them.

Usually, it is better for this runner to sit in and keep on the inside track line, covering as little ground as possible, getting as much good trail as possible and hoping the speed will not be too fast and that he or she can use his or her own speed well near the end.

Front runners often run with all sorts of doubts flitting through their minds about whether they can maintain the speed they are setting, whether it is fast enough or too fast, what is going on behind them – and these doubts can build up nervous tensions which can tie the runner up. When the dreaded and by now expected sprint burst comes from another runner, they are often stranded without a reply and let the rest of the field go by.

Very few important races are won from the front, which confirms that it is wise to stay back if the speed is reasonable. Do not make your own run too soon. Few runners can muster two sprints of more than 100 metres in the one race so it is much better to conserve your energy, both mentally and physically, for the one concerted burst for the tape when you can afford to let everything go.

Twenty years ago, when most distance runners lacked the endurance that is common to top runners today, a runner like Russia's KUTZ could put in a series of windsprints of about 50 metres during a 5,000 metres race and have the opposition gasping for breath and demoralised. You cannot be sure of this tactic any more. Some runners may fall off the pace if subjected to a series of sprints but the majority, if they have done their homework, will absorb them just as easily as the runner applying them.

To run well tactically requires fine control and pace judgement. Too often, runners go off too fast for their ability simply because someone else has done so and they are foolish enough to follow. They get themselves into a large oxygen debt too early and find themselves paying the price near the end of the race.

If the runner is a stamina type who must use endurance to win, it is sometimes worth the gamble to make the early pace fast, provided the wind is not too strong, and hope that faster runners with less stamina will be foolish enough to follow. If they are experienced runners, the chances are they will not and, in this situation, it is sometimes possible to have a breather and then go again.

Study the opposition as much as you can, both locally and in other areas, and find out everything you can about their various strengths and weaknesses. You should even take notes for future reference. You may read about runners from other countries and discount them; but you never know when you are going to find yourself in the same race with one of them. If you have then forgotten what it was you read, you could be penalising yourself, either by failing to exploit a weakness you should have remembered or playing into your rival's hands by running exactly the kind of race he or she likes to run.

You must aim to run every race to cause your opponents the utmost problems. Always remember that the shortest way to the finish is on the inside track edge – every time you get away from it you are increasing the distance you have to run. The wise runners tuck in close to the inside and move out only to pass another runner or to position themselves for the final kick.

In most 800-metre races, the runners cover the first 300 metres in lanes and then break. At this point, you usually see the runners from the outside lanes cutting sharply across to the inside, losing six or more metres because they have not thought. If they aimed for the next inside corner, they would save themselves valuable metres of running they could often do with at the end of the race.

Another habit is for runners to suddenly put in bursts from positions in the middle of the field, take up another trailing position and drift back through the field again. It is a total waste of effort; if you intend to make a move in a race, put some purpose into it and, having achieved your goal, do not let it go again.

There are countless examples of races in which athletes should have or could have won or at least run better races but did not because of tactical mistakes or unintelligent running.

Dave BEDFORD'S 1971 European 10,000 metres championship race in Helsinki was one of them. Before the race, Swedish physiologists who tested him for fitness said he had an oxygen uptake of 87 ml a kilogram, one of the highest, if not THE highest yet recorded. This led to statements that BEDFORD was more-or-less unbeatable, which, physically, perhaps he was. The experts, however, did not take account of other factors which influence a race – like tactics.

BEDFORD was a front runner, used to running his opposition into the ground, getting clear about halfway, and then continuing on to victory unchallenged. Unfortunately for him, this race included runners who had prepared well and could now match his speed in the first 5,000 metres and stay close to him all the way.

BEDFORD is also not the most economical of runners. When he found himself out in front but not clear of the field, it was apparent that nervous tension began to tie him up. At the bell, several runners sprinted past him. They finished with a 53-second last lap, which left BEDFORD floundering behind them.

The winner, VAATAINEN, of Finland, never ran anywhere near as fast as BEDFORD'S best but, tactically, he was the master on the day. I believe that if BEDFORD had not tried to run this fine field into the ground early but had settled into a strong, steady pace, using the last 5,000 metres to apply the pressure, he would not have tied up as he did and would probably have fared much better.

BEDFORD'S world record for 10,000 metres stands as proof of his undoubted ability but it is significant, if unfortunate, that he did not run like that in important competitions.

The 1964 Tokyo Olympic steeplechase, won by Belgium's Gaston ROELANTS, was one of the finest tactical races I have seen. ROELANTS was noted for starting fast and running the field into the ground early, rather like BEDFORD. But, in the Tokyo semi-finals, ROELANTS began to tire after 2,000 metres and did not look as fit as he had previously. Then, when the final field lined up two days later and the gun was fired, ROELANTS did not go to the front as he usually did. It was obvious that the rest of the runners were confused by this and were at a loss what to do next.

So, instead of the pace being fast early as it normally was with ROELANTS in the field, it was slow. Nobody was anxious to take over the ROELANT'S mantle and lead, so everyone muddled along in confusion, reluctant to force the pace until, with 1,000 metres gone, ROELANTS suddenly streaked in to the lead and began running as he usually did at the beginning of a race. He completely surprised the others and gained a good lead which he was able to hold until the finish.

It seemed to me that ROELANTS, on the experience of the semi-final, realised that if he ran his usual race out front, he would be tiring before the finish. He calculated that he could stand the pace for only 2,000 metres, so he planned his personal race from there. It was a switch of tactics that his opponents neither expected nor could counter.

Murray HALBERG'S 5,000 metres win in the 1960 Rome Olympics was an example of hard-way tactics. The plan was simply that he would jump the field with three laps to go and run himself right out to stay in front. It was, we reasoned, the only way of making sure he would win. The HALBERG guts did the rest.

The theory for this tactic was based on some things that had impressed themselves on me since my early days of training. First, whatever exercise you give your body, it will adapt to becoming more efficient at performing it. If you keep running over a certain distance, your body becomes accustomed to that distance. Initial weaknesses vanish, a smooth flowing action develops – but change the distance and the tempo and rhythm are disturbed.

HALBERG went to Rome as a 5,000 metres man who had run a great many three-mile and 5,000-metre time trials at near his best speed to condition him to run strongly for that critical race distance. He was competing against interval-trained athletes, conditioned to run fast over distances from 200 to 600 metres, with rest periods. In other words, they were accustomed to running fast in bursts and then resting; HALBERG was trained to run strongly all the way.

There is also, in most races, a weak spot – the third lap in the mile, the third last lap in the three miles, for instance.

Interval-trained athletes need that rest because their bodies are conditioned to expect it and to more-or-less gather themselves for the final effort.

It is also an interesting point that most three-milers belong to one of two types – the natural miler or the six-miler. The miler finds the early pace well within their capacity, so much so that in the nervous tension of a big race most are inclined to go too fast too early. They are blowing up between $1\frac{3}{4}$ and $2\frac{1}{4}$ miles and are then vulnerable. The six-miler, a stayer, finds the early pace a little difficult to cope with and, about the time the miler is beginning to sag, is wondering if he can hang on to the pace to the finish.

So there is in the three miles and the 5,000 metres, a moment of indecision and reluctance, a psychological moment for the prepared runner to strike. HALBERG had already pulled the same break successfully in the 1958 Empire Games in Cardiff.

I told HALBERG that when the field hesitated with three laps left, he would actually feel the pace slacken and should immediately show his strength with a 60-second lap to break the field. He sensed it all right, applied the pressure and 400 metres later had an 80 metres break on the field. He had only to hold on for two more laps and the gold medal was his.

The last time I won the New Zealand marathon title in Auckland, I used the weather tactically to upset my opposition. The prerace favourite, RICHARDS, was from Christchurch, a much cooler city than Auckland and the day of the race was a typical Auckland one with high humidity.

RICHARDS had run 2:30 for the marathon, which was good running in 1955, but I reasoned that the Auckland heat would get at him. So I cracked on the pace for three or four miles, dragging the field after me, and then eased back out of it. The chance I took paid off. The field went on at the too-fast pace and, with six miles left, I was lying seventh and giving RICHARDS a lead of about a mile.

But I was fresher than he was and I wound up and actually ran the last mile in five minutes while he struggled over it in eight. I passed him and covered the last lap to the finish before he began on it. The heat and humidity had completely drained him during the last few miles because the early speed had eaten too deeply into his reserves.

If a runner is confident that he or she is going to be difficult to beat, it pays to keep the information as secret as possible. As mentioned earlier, I was advising Richard TAYLER in his preparation for the 10,000 metres race in the 1974 Commonwealth Games in Christchurch. His training had been interrupted by illness and a pulled leg muscle and he had lost some of his track training but it was apparent when he ran a 13:40 5,000 metres time trial with consummate ease ten days before the 10,000 that he was going to be hard to beat.

The Press were trying to get all the news they could about the prospects of the runners and, fortunately, Dave BEDFORD was getting the lion's share of the publicity. This suited us, as it kept the pressure right off TAYLER. His best 10,000 to that stage was only 28:24, which did not impress anyone very much, but we knew he was in better form than he had ever been and, as a runner with a 2:15 marathon and a sub-four minute mile, he had both the stamina and the speed to win, provided he ran a sensible, even-paced race and kept out of trouble.

We all knew how the black Africans would run – all over the track, up to the front, drop back, run round the leaders again to upset them and so on – and, because BEDFORD was also a man who liked to be in front, we guessed there would be a fair amount of shoving and jostling during the race's early stages. So I told TAYLER to sit back while this happened and move up only when the leaders had settled down and some of them had dropped off the pace.

I was not wrong. Both BEDFORD and the other English runner, BLACK, tried footing it with the Africans and got several checks. These seemed to upset BEDFORD more than they did BLACK. I was sitting with the English coach, so I asked him why he had not warned the two Englishmen to keep clear of the Africans until they settled. He admitted that he should have done that.

At 5,000 metres, TAYLER was about 60 metres behind the leaders and looked as though he was out of contention but, once the leaders settled down and the hot early pace took its toll, he gradually picked up the four leaders and trailed them.

With two laps to go, BLACK took off but he had little chance with TAYLER, who not only had better speed but fine endurance. The New Zealander picked him off with a sustained sprint from 300 metres out and won by a good 60 metres. His 27:46 was a record for the race and TAYLER'S best by about 40 seconds. BEDFORD, having made too much use of himself in the early jousting, was nowhere.

Another race that was run almost exactly as we planned it was the 1964 Tokyo Olympics 1,500 metres final, in which I was fortunate enough to have two runners, Peter SNELL and John DAVIES. We talked over our tactics the night before the final – I never discuss races with the athletes on the day they are held because I believe they are better left to their own devices. Tensions can be introduced unnecessarily by talking about a race and trying to give last-minute advice.

We felt SNELL'S prospects were great but that DAVIES would not be among the medals if he got caught up in a sprint finish because his speed was not really good enough. There were many faster men in the field. He had tried a sprint finish from 250 metres in the semi-final and had nearly given me heart failure because everyone else had the same idea and DAVIES was four lanes wide on the final bend trying to outsprint faster men. He managed to scramble into a qualifying fourth place – but only just.

We did not want this to happen again so we decided that, at 800 metres to go, DAVIES would take over the pace and SNELL would try to run on his shoulder so they could dictate the situation. Being a long-striding runner, SNELL would be diffficult to pass and would force any overtaking runner out two or three lanes.

We considered the danger man was the American Dyrol BURLESON. He had drawn the inside lane, so we planned that DAVIES would match BURLESON'S early pace and keep him on the inside. We expected the Frenchman Michel BERNARD to do the early front running but, because he was interval-trained, we did not expect him to last three hard races.

It happened as though we had told everyone beforehand what they were to do. BERNARD took the lead. BURLESON was inside DAVIES. With 700 to go, BERNARD began to flag and DAVIES shifted quickly to the lead. But then, before SNELL could get up on the outside, another runner grabbed the place we had reserved for him and SNELL got himself into a box.

With 250 metres left, SNELL took off as planned – well, almost. He had to get out of his boxed position first but, instead of dropping back and going round the field as he had done from a similar box in the semi-final and as any runner might be expected to do, he stuck out his right arm like a traffic signal and the obliging Englishman John WHETTON made a gap for him. DAVIES by then had his ears back, sprinting as hard as he could go.

As they swept into the straight, with SNELL leading, the Englishman ran round DAVIES, forcing him to change course and stop a little; this let Josef ODLOZIL, of Czechoslovakia through and though DAVIES finished fast, he was nipped out of second to SNELL by a few centimetres.

BURLESON never got out of the bunch. A few years later I overheard him telling someone in discussing the race. *"If I could have got out I would have won."* I have often wondered if he knew how he got boxed in the first place.

This was a successful tactical race because we knew the runners we were racing against and the type of training they used. It was interesting too because, despite the calm with which he handled the last 400 metres, including the box, SNELL actually ran them in 53.2 seconds – the last 300 in 38.6 seconds.

You often meet runners you know little or nothing about. If there are heats and semi-finals, it pays to have your coach or a running ally who is not competing look the field over and estimate the capabilities of the unknown quantities. This is usually necessary at the Olympics and big internationals because there you often come up against other runners for the first time.

You can also test these runners out in heats or semi-finals by running the race with a sharp finishing sprint to gauge their speed. Or you can make it a long sustained sprint, though the others will not always take the bait and do what you want them to do, and you have to be pretty confident yourself. But it is interesting that once a runner lets go a sprint, the others follow unless the standard of the field is poor. Some runners mix the pace continually and they need watching because, if you have not got good pace judgement, you can be fooled into an unnecessary series of windsprints.

Pass other runners only on the straights, unless there is no option but to go on a bend. Keep to the pole line as much as possible – the more you leave it, the longer your race becomes. Try to keep the pace as even and economical as you can; the runner who sprints in the middle stages is not likely to be sprinting at the end.

Go into every race with a plan in mind. Whether the race goes according to that plan depends on many factors, but if all considerations are made and logic is used, invariably the runner who plans ahead best will not be caught napping by others' tactics and can quite often call the tune.

Runners today are generally conditioning well and training to be prepared for any eventuality so the use of various tactics is being minimised, though there will always be runners who go for surprises. The levelling out in training, however, means that, more and more, the ultimate tactical weapon is that finishing sprint.

The 1956 Olympics were the last to be dominated by the interval-trained middle and distance athletes. With the dismal failure of the West Germans in Melbourne, Dr. GERSHLER, who, with Dr. RIENDELL, was mainly responsible for the development of this training method, lost face with the German athletic authorities, coaches and athletes and his fame waned all over the world.

In the next four years, Australian and New Zealand runners, training on marathon-type conditioning, came into form, eclipsing the efforts of the athletes still using the older methods. ELLIOT, THOMAS, POWER and LINCOLN from Australia and Neville SCOTT and HALBERG from my group dominated international competitions between 1957 and 1959.

The 1960 Olympics proved the soundness of our technique. SNELL took the 800, Elliot the 1,500, Halberg the 5,000 and Barry MAGEE ran third in the marathon with the fastest time then recorded by a white man. This led to an interesting conference in West Germany to debate the merits of our system, followed by a general switch in training in several countries.

HALBERG won his event because he had better co-ordination; SNELL'S strength was his ability to combine speed with better stamina than his opponents possessed, even though he was an international novice; MAGEE, who was running only his third marathon, was like Abebe BIKILA and the second-placed Moroccan, A. RHADI, an endurance-trained runner with a high oxygen uptake level. All three had the ability to understand and apply tactics.

9   Body Temperature, Electrolytes, and Running

Body temperature varies throughout the body. It is lost by physical processes and by physiological factors which enable the blood to be cooled as it flows through near the skin and by providing water for cooling the skin by vaporisation.

When the air temperature is low, the blood vessels of the skin contract to diminish heat loss; when the temperature is high, or when exercise produces excess body heat, they dilate. More perspiration is secreted and evaporative heat loss is greater. The more you exercise, the more blood flows through the outer skin area and the more you perspire.

Strenuous exercise creates a demand for more blood for the muscles and for more to flow to the skin for cooling; the warmer the atmosphere, the greater the demand becomes. This pressure can exceed the capacity of the heart to increase cardiac output, causing nausea, dizziness and even heat-stroke.

If you are not accustomed to exercising strenuously in heat, you are immediately exposed to these progressive problems: heat cramps through excessive loss of salt and water, which leads to neuromuscular breakdown; heat exhaustion, through circulatory inadequacy caused by dehydration; and, at the worst, heat-stroke, a condition serious enough to kill because the temperature-controlling centre of the brain becomes deranged.

You can adapt yourself to exercising in the heat by carefully controlling and gradually lengthening exercise periods while the circulation of blood to the arterioles in the skin improves in response to the stimulation you are giving it.

Marathon runners are often required to race in hot conditions in which body temperatures rises to extremes and dehydration is excessive. If they have been training in the heat, they can usually handle these conditions quite well but those unaccustomed to heat rarely finish and are often in a distressed state of fatigue for some time afterwards.

Jim PETERS' marathon run in the 1954 Empire Games in Vancouver is probably the classic example of a fine marathon runner who came close to death through dehydration and circulatory failure because he was not prepared to compete in high heat.

People taking their first sauna bath usually feel extremely hot and even faint in temperatures of around 80°C but, over a conditioning period of a few weeks, can comfortably withstand temperatures up to 120°C.

The body's temperature-regulating mechanism is most efficient, as I have proved during marathons in which I have been suffering from the effects of heat. Instead of using the customary sponge, I would up-end a bucket of water over myself. The cooling effect was almost instantaneous and allowed me to run freely again. I found I could run my regular marathon-training courses ten to fifteen minutes faster on cool days, which proved the degree to which the metabolism is taxed in hot conditions.

I have seen athletes trying to reduce weight by running distances on hot days in heavy clothing. They will certainly deplete their bodies of water and minerals but, because they are limiting the volume of running they could do by overdressing, and they will not be burning as much fat as they might hope. A few hours after stopping, they will have replaced most of the liquid they lost and their weight will be pretty much where it was earlier.

If they wore less clothing to keep the body temperature down and then ran farther and more intensely, they would be using up some of the fat in their bodies.

Another factor they overlook is that heavy clothing, by causing higher body temperatures, draws blood from the working muscles to the skin for emergency cooling, so the efficiency of the working muscles is reduced. Since it is necessary to do as large a volume of running as possible to develop general cardiac efficiency, anything that gets in the way is to be avoided. Wear only the clothing that is necessary; any more retards movement, overheats the body and reduces running's benefits.

In high temperatures, even near 40°C, you can continue steady running for an hour or more, as long as the humidity is also high, and the moisture perspired can remain on the skin surface to help cooling. If the humidity is low, the perspiration evaporates quickly and creates conditions for dehydration.

When I tried a run in Tucson, Arizona, the temperature was 38°C and the humidity less than 20 percent. I lasted about 20 minutes and then decided I should stop. But, for six weeks in Maracaibo, Venezuela, at sea level and 10 degrees from the equator, I trained regularly for at least an hour a day. The temperature was always high – between 38 and 50°C – and I ran in the middle of the day, when everyone else was having a siesta, on the tarmac of an old airport. I could even do speed training for a full hour. I suffered no ill effects because the humidity was always near 90 percent and I was always wet with perspiration. I followed this programme to accustom myself to the heat so that I could sleep more easily at night when it remained extremely hot.

A study of runners after the 1968 Boston marathon and the United States Olympic marathon trial showed body temperatures were up to 41°C, and wider research revealed that it was not unusual for temperatures to be higher than 40°C after races of beyond six miles (ten kilometres). It was considered then that part of the distress seen during the final phase of a distance race might well be attributable to the stress of excessive body heat on the nervous system – a state of hyperthermia.

Little can be done about the environment but it is obvious that the runner must slow his or her pace to minimise the detrimental effects of a warm, sunny day. Most runners fail to allow for the weather hazards when they are racing. Taking fluids frequently helps the body's air conditioning system; every ten to fifteen minutes is desirable, according to some researchers.

The first symptoms of hyperthermia occur at about 40°C body heat: throbbing pressure in the temples, cold sensation over the trunk. If the temperature climbs a little higher, muscular weakness, disorientation and loss of equilibrium follow; higher still, and diminished sweating and loss of consciousness occur.

At the point where you experience that throbbing in the temples allied with chills, you should stop immediately and try to lower your body temperature with cold fluids or cool showers. To continue is dangerous.

The opposite applies when you train in sub-zero temperatures. If there is moisture in the air when temperatures are 20 to 40°C below, it can become impossible to train because you risk icing your lungs. But, if the humidity is below 20 percent, you can train in those temperatures for hours, as long as the wind is not too severe and you are well wrapped up. As I explained in the chapter on clothing, I trained in Finland in two tracksuits which gave me a cushion of body-warmed air to run in. A woollen hat, muffler, gloves and socks protected every other part of me except my cheeks.

Remember the formula if you live, run or train in an area of temperature extremes: when the temperature is high, the humidity needs to be high; when the temperature is low, the humidity should also be low. If any other combination prevails, be careful of running into trouble. Limit your training.

The hazards are surprisingly real and too many have been caught by them. Recently, in bush not far from New Zealand's capital, Wellington, three young runners died of exposure. They ran a short distance into the bush following a regular jogger's trail, but encountered a sudden dramatic temperature drop, rain and hail. They were lightly clad and were almost immediately in difficulties from which they could not recover, because no-one was near to help them. They were dead before they knew what had happened to them.

The human body is a machine which works at 37°C. The other areas can get much colder but the vital organs must stay at that constant temperature. If, in cold, wet and windy conditions, the core begins to cool and the cooling is not immediately checked, you will suffer mental deterioration, loss of co-ordination, unconsciousness and total failure of breathing and circulation. Within 30 minutes of the first symptoms, you can be dead.

Check the progressive warning signs: tiredness, cold or exhaustion; lack of interest, lethargy; clumsiness, stumbling or falling; slurring speech, difficulty in seeing; irrational behaviour; obvious distress; the cessation of shivering, despite the cold; collapse and unconsciousness; coma.

It sounds unreal and a sense of unreality is one of the warning signs. If you feel any of the early symptoms while you are running in cold, wet and windy weather or note them in a companion, you must act immediately to prevent further heat loss, begin warming and try to prevent loss of consciousness. Do not bash on and hope for the best because that can cause the rapid onset of more serious stages. You must get out of the wind, get dry clothing, warm drinks and, essentially, send for expert help.

The best advice, of course, is to be adequately equipped with clothing to protect you against a sudden fall in conditions. And bear in mind that heat loss from the head is high – a fact often overlooked.

Over-breathing or hyperventilation is another unusual hazard. What happens is that, due to nervous tension, a person starts to overbreathe and blows off too much carbon dioxide. This gas is the stimulus to breathe and as the level in the blood drops, it causes biochemical changes which can lead to giddiness, pins and needles, rapid beating of the heart and a feeling of dread.

With most of the carbon dioxide breathed out, there is not enough gas in the blood to stimulate the breathing centres, breathing may stop and the victim may feel no desire to take a further breath. Then, because no oxygen is taken in, the level of this gas reaching the brain drops and this can lead to unconsciousness.

Then, as the level of carbon dioxide produced by the tissues builds up again, the breathing resumes and the person regains consciousness. Sometimes, the altered calcium metabolism in this phenomenon causes muscles to tense and twitch and hyperventilation can be mistaken for an epileptic seizure.

The remedies are to force a person under attack to slow down breathing or to breathe in and out of a paper bag, which forces him or her to re-breathe carbon dioxide and restores the balance.

However, exercise creates a surplus of carbon dioxide and uses up oxygen so it is a phenomenon not likely to be experienced by athletes except in rare circumstances. The outpouring of lactic acid into the blood contributes to heavy breathing and breathlessness but, by decomposing bicarbonate, also causes a temporary increase in the output of carbon dioxide.

Training in a warm climate or perspiring profusely, you have to replace minerals as well as lost water. In long-duration competition, such as the marathon, you should take liquids regularly before any effects of dehydration are felt.

Electrolyte drinks are now available – I recommend you take them at half the suggested strengths – which replenish lost minerals, but check that the one you buy contains calcium, magnesium and potassium. The reasons are discussed in the next chapter.

10   Foods, Fads and Fancies

So you are in peak condition, training and running well, feeling strong – and also tired because you cannot sleep? Your muscles cramp, twitch and tremble and will not let you. The probability is that your running and eating do not balance each other correctly and you are into a mineral deficiency, particularly of calcium, magnesium and potassium, because that is what running takes out of you and what you have to be sure to put back.

Your body contains about 3 lb (1.5 kg) of calcium – a lot more than any other mineral in your body – and though most of it is in your bones and teeth the remaining one-tenth of one percent is vital. Without it, your muscles could not contract. If the mechanism that regulates the level of that small but precious amount of calcium is so precise that, if the amount drops a microgram too low, calcium is immediately taken from the bones to make up the deficit.

That is why you can unknot muscle cramps by taking extra calcium. Exercise has been found to decrease the amount of calcium lost through general physical degeneration and ageing but when you are in the running business it is important to replenish even the smallest losses.

An American study on 200 insomniacs discovered that if they took 500 mg of magnesium each day, they slept and, on waking, tiredness had vanished in 99 percent of the subjects. Anxiety and tension decreased.

Magnesium is a natural tranquilliser and also quietens jumpy muscles and nerves. Enough magnesium results in relaxed muscles; too little and they twitch and tremble. It also aids the digestion of protein, fat and carbohydrates. Hours of endurance exercise drains your body of magnesium, so you have to make sure it goes back each day.

If you do not sweat when you are exercising, you probably need potassium and those who do sweat and take salt tablets need double doses. A professor at the University of Texas Southwestern Medical School, Dr James KNOCHEL, found that 50 per cent of of people hospitalised for heat-stroke after intense exercise were potassium depleted. Many of them had taken salt tablets, which forced potassium out of the body. That loss, added to what they were losing through sweat, caused a severe potassium deficiency and all its symptoms: nausea, muscle weakness, cramps, irritability and, finally, total collapse. You do not need to replace salt lost in sweat but you do need to replace potassium.

So where do you get mineral replacements? Most electrolyte drinks, as mentioned in the previous chapter, provide all three, but the other sources are:

Calcium: It has been calculated that if you get 100 grams of protein a day you need also to have 1,000 mg of calcium, because protein forces calcium out of the body. Three glasses of milk will give you that amount; a cup of cottage cheese has 230 mg; an ounce of Swiss cheese 262; eight ounces of yoghurt 294; sardines and salmon (with bones) are loaded; a cup of collard or turnip greens more than 250.

Magnesium: Whole grains, soybeans, nuts, green leafy vegetables, fruits and blackstrap molasses all contain magnesium. But better than these is dolomite, a preparation from powdered dolomite limestone, which also delivers calcium and in the exact proportions nature intended. Your aim should be 350 to 500 mg a day.

Potassium: A medium-sized banana has 500 mg; other good sources are oranges, tomatoes, cabbage, celery, carrots, grapefruit, apples, beans and fish.

Many athletes switch their normal diet before an important competition or at other times during their training without thinking about the possible effects. I have known a lot of them to complain later that they felt really bad during competition, performed poorly and realised too late what they had done. If you want to experiment with your diet, because you feel it may not be providing the right balance of food, do so but investigate the subject first and reserve your experiment for periods when the wrong reaction will not affect your training or racing too severely.

In countries with a high standard of living, most athletes can maintain a balanced diet with few or no problems, though in universities and other establishments where food is prepared in large quantities and the catering is less for athletic appetites than for non-athletic appetites, certain vitamin and mineral deficiences can be expected. The same is true of the processed convenience foods which abound today.

You can take vitamin tablets and mineral tablets but they are largely only a supplement and should be relied on only in situations where you cannot control the selection and preparation of your food. Always remember that, as long as you are training, your vitamin and mineral requirement is higher than normal, and defiencies could cause a lot of breakdown in your body – but this is not a licence to swallow every tablet you can obtain.

The only athletes I trained who needed any tablets were a few who were deficient in iron. New Zealand in those days had ample fresh vegetables; most of us grew our own and there was no lack of meat and other primary produce. Now, more processed food is being eaten and this evolution has to be weighed carefully. Every runner should evaluate what he or she is eating and what he or she needs. If a number of people sit down to identical meals, some will assimilate more minerals from it than others; some will get full value, some will suffer from deficiencies. This is an individual reaction, so it must be approached individually. There is no mass solution.

I honestly doubt that my athletes would have run any faster if they had taken vitamin tablets but I have seen American athletes carrying bags full of multi-coloured vitamin pills. An American university physiologist told me he believed vitamins were only of value to young babies and children up to four or five. After that, he said, young athletes who had good food sources available were wasting their time with tablet-taking because they achieved little more than coloured urine.

For runners who have accepted my marathon-type conditioning method, an increased calorie intake is necessary. You cannot do this efficiently by eating more of the bulky foods; they are harder to digest and place extra work on the digestive system. Certainly cereals, bread and potatoes are the best source of carbohydrate, but there is a limit to how much bulk an athlete can take, particularly in periods leading up to major competitions. I suggest using honey, because it is basically nothing but energy, and will give the athlete all the energy needed.

What you are aiming for is to store blood sugars in the liver and bloodstream for use during competition or training, and, as a supplement to normal sources, honey is an easily handled ideal.

It is not wise to take sugar or food within three hours of competition because the insulin in the blood is increased and this retards the release of energy. However, if yours begin taking extra sugar while you are running, the reaction is different.

The controversial B_{15}, discovered by Ernst. T. KREBS, jun., is not a vitamin but a non-toxic food supplement found in natural form in many foods we no longer eat enough of, including lentils, broad beans, almonds, cashew nuts, millet grain, non-hybrid buckwheat and in the pits of apples, pears, quinces, apricots, peaches, plums, nectarines and prunes. These are not carcinogenic as a vociferous element of the medical profession would have us believe.

Natural foods, whenever you can eat them, are the ultimate in training because as well as the natural balance of vitamins and minerals, they also supply the enzymes needed to activate them.

If you put a potato in the ground, it will grow, but a cooked potato will not. So beware of overcooking and, if you can, provide yourself with a juice extractor. Use it to juice vegetables as well as fruits, particularly cabbage and celery, and drink the juice immediately for maximum vitamin, mineral and enzyme benefit. The modern juice extractor is worth its weight in gold to everyone, not just the practising athlete.

In 1970, I had the good fortune to meet Professor CURATIN, of Champagne, Illinois, one of the world's experts on exercise nutrition. He told me then he was worried about the future of the American nation as a whole because of its intake of preservatives, colourings and flavourings, its lack of roughage and the destruction of vital minerals and vitamins in its method of food preparation and presentation.

All round the world where food is grown, the ground is becoming deficient in trace elements; artifical fertilisers are being forced in to promote food and animal growth and they often destroy a plant's ability to absorb trace elements from the soil; more and more people are unable to get fresh fruit and vegetables.

All this has forced us to consider food supplements as an alternative, particularly when we are making heavy demands on our bodies. The gluconates are one of the best-known forms of supplement but recent research has found that orotates, the vitamin B_{13} mineral salts, can be employed as mineral transporters, because they are highly efficient in delivering a selected mineral to the exact parts of the body which most need it. They are now being used for the treatment of many chronic disorders and could equally assist athletes in specific mineral replacement.

In practise, I found that it was highly beneficial to eat about 200 mg of glucose or honey in the 36 hours before a competition. When I later visited the Soviet Union, a Russian physiologist discussed this prerace honey intake with me and confirmed that they had proved scientifically that 200 mg was the ideal amount because either more or less gave poor results. My athletes ate the glucose type of barley sugar but I now prefer honey, which is a fructose and easier to digest.

It is important to remember that the food you eat the day before you race is the food that will provide most of the energy for the race and help in your recovery; so forget about the competition-day steak as having any value. It is the steak you eat the day before that will count.

On race-day, eat at breakfast of cereals, light-cooked (not hard-boiled) eggs, tea, coffee or any other drink you like; just avoid a heavy or fatty breakfast and give it plenty of time to digest. Lunch should be mainly carbohydrate – various meals meet this need without being too heavy. Honey sandwiches, of course, are ideal; so are baked beans.

On the morning of the marathon or long distance race, you can be a little more casual because your running is going to be slightly anaerobic. And, if the race begins at 9 or 10 in the morning, or earlier, it is too much to expect the athlete to be up early enough to have his or her last food three hours before going to the starter. A carbohydrate breakfast with honey on toast and the drink of your choice is fine as late as two hours or even an hour before the run.

It is a question of finding out what suits you individually, but it is not overly important. Many athletes would be better if they did not eat at all. If they suffer from prerace tensions, food could upset their digestive systems. The basic formula is to have protein to help recovery but confine yourself to carbohydrates on race-day.

Drinking alcohol within twelve hours of a race is unwise. The alcohol is absorbed by the red cells and precludes the absorption of oxygen. But you can take other liquids right up to race start and even if you can hear the liquid sloshing around inside, there will be no discomfort.

A carbohydrate boosting programme to raise the level of glycogen stored in the muscles has been adopted by many middle and distance runners. The theory is that you have a long hard training run seven days before the event, which depresses the blood sugar level; then, for three days, you keep the level down by eating almost exclusively fats or proteins which is supposed to increase the ability of the muscles to absorb sugar. Training runs are light and easy. From the afternoon of the fourth day, you switch to a carbohydrate-enriched diet until the race, the body responding by storing up abnormal quantities of glycogen in the muscles, perhaps as much as three or four times the normal value. The theory also says that you will feel very tired during the non-carbohydrate period but you must stick to diet. I do not advise runners to use this method. If they must, they should try it out before a race which is not too important.

In aerobic exercise, energy comes from a ratio of 48 percent carbohydrate, 48 percent fat acids and 4 percent protein, or thereabouts. In anaerobic exercise, the ratio is about 60 percent carbohydrate, 25 percent fat acids and 15 percent protein. So there is an increase in the burning of carbohydrate in competition calling for anaerobic effort. This is the fact that has led athletes to try to increase the amount of glycogen in the body to offset the quick depletion of their energy; but the theory that the body can store extra glycogen through this method is debatable and it can also lead to other problems.

There is a need for fat acids and proteins; if these are insufficient, the runner on the carbohydrate diet can suffer dizziness and greater muscle soreness.

My advice is: if you want to build blood sugars to the maximum, take a light laxative six days before your race so that your bowels are loosened a little, not a lot. Eat the meals you normally eat but, two days before the competition, eat up to 200 grams of glucose or honey.

Invariably, the effect of the laxative is to stimulate the liver into readily making the maximum amount of glycogen that the body can contain and the extra sugars taken in the last two days will add the final touches, giving an abundance of energy without upsetting the balance of fat acid, protein and carbohydrate. Supercompensation is rather like trying to put five litres into a four-litre bucket.

The French physiologist, Claude BERNARD, discovered that the glucose content of the blood entering the liver after a meal had a much higher concentration of sugar than the blood leaving the liver. Between meals, liver glycogen was reconverted into glucose, so that the concentration of glycogen in the blood leaving the liver was much higher than in the blood entering the liver. He also found that the liver maintains the glucose concentration more or less constantly during the day.

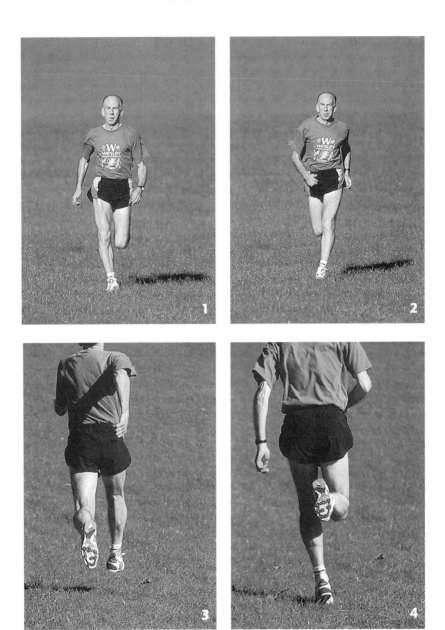

Running tall – fast relaxed running with good knee lift, high back heel and leg extension.

Stretching and suppling: These exercises are important before and after athletic effort. First, to stretch muscles and tendons easily and stimulate blood flow; afterwards, to ease muscles which have been under stress and to help the body to get rid of any wastes generated by running.

Pulling up on the raised back foot, full back and forward leg swings, across-the-body toe touching and rhythmic circular hip rotation, all shown here, will work on all parts of the body and limbs.

High knees: sprinters use this exercise. All runners should. Forward momentum is slow as the knees are raised high and fast in an exaggerated almost on-the-spot running action. ➔

Striding: the objective of striding, which is used in sprint training, is to lift the knees high and take long strides while forcing the arms through and driving hard off the back foot.

Fast, relaxed running. Note the back leg drive, perfect body angle and arm movements.

11   Injury Prevention and Cure

People who run on the balls of their feet and cannot get their heels down first when running aerobically are more susceptible to foot troubles than the runners who land nearly flat footed, touching the heel somewhat on the outer edge and then rolling forward onto the ball of the foot and toes. This is because, when you are running aerobically, the body's centre of gravity takes longer to pass over the lead foot, so more friction is developed when the ball of the foot hits ahead of the heel, resulting in a braking action which can cause blistering, damaged or blue toe nails, metatarsal damage and shin splints.

This foot fault is caused by tighter leg tendons, by bad practice or by the individual's inability to run any other way; whatever the reason, training should be on grass or sand as much as possible to lessen the friction and keep problems at bay.

Knee trouble often arises during conditioning work because the upper front leg muscles and sinews are too tight and stressed. These quadriceps must be strengthened by uphill running or by doing squats or other stretching exercises.

Ill-fitting or worn-down shoes can cause knee and hip trouble as mentioned earlier. You should check your shoes every week: if you are running correctly with balance, the main wear will be on the back outer edge of the heel, the outside of the forepart and slightly at the toe, and it should be even on both shoes. If not, it could indicate you are running with tight arm or shoulder muscles, badly fitting shoes or even with a skeletal defect which makes you run lopsided. This is not necessarily dangerous but it is a good reason for keeping your shoes in good order.

The shoes are your main cost in running but it pays to look after them and not try to economise by letting them wear too far. A few millimetres off part of the sole alters the stress of running on your ankles, knees and hips and could cause unexpected problems.

Achilles' tendon trouble is usually caused during resistance work when you could be trying to build powerful muscles without doing enough suppling and stretching exercises. The importance of full extension of muscles and sinews must be appreciated. A man working with weights seldom gets full extension on his legs until he goes outside and sprints – and at just the moment when he is not ready for it.

Hamstring trouble is caused by leg-speed running with muscles and sinews not stretched and conditioned equally. Often the quadriceps are more powerful than the hamstrings so, when you pull the leg through fast with a high knee lift using full quadricep power, you risk pulling the weaker hamstring muscles. You have to use the full range of calisthenics for the full range of movement and you must concentrate on all the running exercises we have built into the schedules.

Pulled muscles are simply a breakdown of the sheathing around muscle fibres and tearing of the fibres themselves. Poor warming-up and poor conditioning are major contributors to the damage; but it can happen even if all things are done properly because the stress of using these muscles for long periods can cause a breaking down of muscle tissue. Even the athlete who takes every precaution can experience the trouble under the most perfect conditions – but is a whole lot less vulnerable than the careless athlete.

When a muscle is pulled, you can put your finger accurately on the spot. There will be internal bleeding there and you must stop it. Ice or cold water are most effective. Ice draws cortisone to the area which stimulates enzyme function to improve circulation. Treat it this way for three days before you begin massage; by then, scar tissue will have formed around the affected area. The massage helps to get rid of excess blood around the tissue and to stimulate food supplies to the injury zone.

In all injury cases, you should go to a qualified physician rather than treat yourself. You could aggravate the damage. Even with stresses of the knee and ankle joints, a physician's advice and treatment is better.

Shin splints are membrane ruptures between the muscle and the bone and often arise because of the jarring of downhill running or overstriding. Shoes that turn up in front and are not, in the true sense, flats can also cause ruptures because they encourage the front of the foot to clap on the road.

You can counter overstriding by building up the front of your shoes a little and you should always be cautious when running downhill. Water therapy or cold packs, followed by heat treatment, can help this injury, though they are the most difficult to overcome.

Water therapy is invaluable for all lower limb injuries. Just get into a tepid pool and kick with a kickboard or simulate the running action while treading water.

Knee cartilage or meniscus trouble is a common problem but can be treated fairly easily if it is not too serious. If you feel a cartilage is giving trouble, you should seek medical attention immediately; the use of an arthroscope, diagnosis is so exact that treatment could be prescribed to leave you running again in days. Leave it and you become an arthritic problem and then you are in real trouble. Even teenagers can have meniscus trouble so no-one should treat telltale twinges lightly.

Injuries to joints and bone wear are invariably caused by poor buffers and jarring on hard surfaces, or by rotation of the joints, possibly by throwing your arms too far across the body. Correct that fault and you may correct the joint problem. If you always run on the same side of the road, you will probably always be running with the same leg effectively slightly longer than the other to compensate for the road camber. You should vary sides to counter this.

Unless you have plenty of good resilient rubber between you and the ground, the shock of each stride can be felt over a wide area of the body and problems can arise in unexpected places – hip aches, low back pain and so on. There are plenty of treatments available these days to remedy these aches and pains but the most effective method is prevention first by inserting padding between you and the ground which gives you a good recoil. Shoes which achieve this may not be cheap to buy but they will be cheap in the long term.

It is far better to prevent than to cure; far easier to get yourself correctly shod, to make sure your running action is balanced, and to do suppling and stretching exercises (five minutes a day should not be too much to spare) than to suffer the injuries, the cost and discomfort of curing them and the loss of time for running.

12   The Schedules

Supplementary to all the following schedules, it is wise to run as many kilometres as possible at easy aerobic effort. This will help you to maintain good general condition, keep improving your endurance and recover from training sessions. Even an extra fifteen minutes of jogging has value.

Regular exercise running on hills will help you in developing and maintaining your speed. Try to fit in some hill springing, uphill running with a driving action and some steep hill or step running whenever you can, but do not overdo it.

The schedules are only for guidance. They give a balanced method of training for a specific event, but they must be treated as flexible to the needs of your age, sex and general condition. Study your reactions to training from day to day and if you feel jaded or suffer from any soreness allow time for recovery.

Never do speed training when your muscles are sore or you are feeling very tired. Just jog easily, irrespective of what is on the schedule for that day's training. You can never do yourself any harm by jogging and it will usually help to overcome the soreness or tiredness. Fast training can lead to injury and will certainly only make you more tired.

Control your training so that you are not racing it, except when full efforts are called for in the schedules. Run strongly and easily in effort, always keeping something in reserve. As you feel improvement, gradually increase your training tempo but never use that reserve.

The instruction 'for as long as possible' on the schedules refers to the period between the finish of the cross-country or road racing season and the start of specialised track preparation training. For convenience, the various training phases are coded A to Z, though not all are used.

SPRINTS

The weekly training for sprinters should incorporate the following:

1. Aerobic running on a regular basis sufficient to raise the maximum steady state and increase endurance to get you through your later sprint training without tiring. This can be done as a separate training sessions or as cooling down runs after other training. Even a 15-minute run is effective.

2. Easy fartlek over easy undulating ground where you can stride out, run fast at times, run a few hilly areas and generally mix in all types of running training. It allows for the gradual increase of the capacity to exercise anaerobically.

3. Hill springing which you should work at all the time for essential ankle flexibility and power. Bouncing up gentle slopes on your toes will gradually develop much power and flexion in the ankles, stretch other leg muscles and tendons and eliminate the risk of strains and pulls. White muscle fibres will develop more efficiency.

4. Running up steep hills benefits the upper leg muscles and you need well-conditioned quadriceps to enable the good knee lift necessary for sprint stride length and speed.

5. Technique training should be done regularly so that faulty running actions do not develop during conditioning. This involves high knee lift, long striding ankle exercise running and running tall at least once a week.

6. Relaxed striding helps you to relax during all your running. Using a following wind, you should stride several times over 150 to 200 metres once a week.

7. Suppling and stretching exercises should be done continually but particularly before fast training. Exercise your whole body this way every day.

8. Hurdling can often improve sprinting ability – and may well disclose a latent hurdling talent.

Note

A – Long aerobic running

B – Easy fartlek running

C – Strong fartlek running

D – Hill springing

E – Steep hills or step running

F – Leg speed

G – Sprint training

H – 45-metre windsprints every 100 metres

J – 100-metre windsprints every 200 metres

K – Repetitions

L – Time trials

M – Pace judgement running

N – Relaxed striding

O – Fast relaxed running

P – High knee-lift exercise

Q – Long striding exercising

R – Running tall exercising

S – Calisthenics

T – Skipping

U – Cycling

V – Swimming

W – Jogging

X – Sprints starts

Y – Hurdles practice

Z – Water jump practice

Sprints – boys and girls

For as long as possible:

Monday	BDE 15 to 30 minutes
Tuesday	PQR and N 200 m x 4
Wednesday	BDE 15 to 30 minutes
Thursday	PQR and N 200 m x 4
Friday	F 100 m x 4-6
Saturday	400 m x 2-3 at $\frac{3}{4}$ effort
Sunday	B 15 to 30 minutes

For six weeks:

Monday	BDE 15 to 30 minutes
Tuesday	PQR 80 m x 2 each
Wednesday	N 200 m x 4-6
Thursday	X 30 m x 4 and O 100 m x 4
Friday	F 100 m x 4-6
Saturday	L 100 m and 200 m or 400 m
Sunday	B 20 to 40 minutes

For four weeks:

Monday	200 m x 2 or 300 m x 1 fast
Tuesday	XGS
Wednesday	L 100 m and 200 m or 400 m
Thursday	H x 8-12
Friday	W 15 to 20 minutes
Saturday	Race 100 m and 200 m or 400 m
Sunday	B 20 to 40 minutes

For four weeks:

Monday	H x 8-12
Tuesday	O 100 m x 4 and X 30 m x 6
Wednesday	L 100 m x 2 and 200 m
Thursday	GS
Friday	W 15 to 20 minutes
Saturday	Race
Sunday	W 20 to 30 minutes

For one week:

Monday	L 300 m x 1
Tuesday	O 100 m x 4
Wednesday	Race 100 m x 2 and 200 m
Thursday	GS
Friday	W 20 minutes
Saturday	Race 100 m and 200 m
Sunday	W 20 to 30 minutes

For one week:

Monday	GS
uesday	B 15 to 20 minutes
Wednesday	L 100 m x 2
Thursday	N 200 m x 2
Friday	W 15 minutes or rest
Saturday	First important race
Sunday	B 15 to 30 minutes

Continuation of racing:

Monday	GS
Tuesday	H x 8-12
Wednesday	Race 100 m and 200 m
Thursday	B 15 to 30 minutes
Friday	N 150 m x 3-4 or rest
Saturday	Race
Sunday	B 15-30 minutes

Sprints – men

For as long as possible:

Monday	BDE $\frac{1}{2}$ hour
Tuesday	PQR and N 300 m x 4
Wednesday	BDE $\frac{1}{2}$ hour
Thursday	PQR and N 300 m x 4
Friday	F 120 m x 10
Saturday	800 m x 3 at $\frac{3}{4}$ effort
Sunday	B one hour

For six weeks:

Monday	BDE $\frac{1}{2}$ hour
Tuesday	PQR 100m each x 3
Wednesday	N 200 m x 8
Thursday	X 30 m x 6 and O 100 m x 6
Friday	F 120 m x 10
Saturday	L 100 m and 200 m or 400 m
Sunday	B one hour

For four weeks:

Monday	300m x 3 or 500 m x 2 fast
Tuesday	XGS
Wednesday	L 100 m and 200 m or 400 m
Thursday	H x 12-16
Friday	W $\frac{1}{2}$ hour
Saturday	Race 100 m and 200 m or 400 m
Sunday	B $\frac{3}{4}$ hour

For four weeks:

Monday	H x 12 or 300 m x 3
Tuesday	O 100 m x 6 and X 30 m x 6
Wednesday	L 100 m and 200 m or 400 m
Thursday	GS
Friday	W $\frac{1}{2}$ hour
Saturday	Race
Sunday	W $\frac{3}{4}$ hour

For one week:

Monday	L 500 m x 2
Tuesday	O 100 m x 6
Wednesday	Race 100 m x 2 and 200 m
Thursday	G and S
Friday	W $\frac{1}{2}$ hour
Saturday	Race 100 m and 200 m or 400 m
Sunday	W $\frac{1}{2}$ hour

For one week:

Monday	G and S
Tuesday	B ½ hour
Wednesday	L 100 m x 2
Thursday	N 200 m x 3
Friday	W ½ hour or rest
Saturday	Race
Sunday	B ½ hour

Continuation of racing:

Monday	S and X
Tuesday	B ½ to ¾ hour
Wednesday	L sprints
Thursday	F 100 m x 6-8
Friday	Rest or jog
Saturday	Race
Sunday	W and N – 200 m x 4-6

400 metres – boys, 13 to 15 years

For as long as possible:

Monday	A 20 to 30 minutes
Tuesday	A 30 to 45 minutes
Wednesday	B 20 to 30 minutes
Thursday	A 30 to 45 minutes
Friday	N 150 m x 6
Saturday	A 30 to 45 minutes
Sunday	B 20 to 30 minutes

For four weeks:

Monday	DE ¼ to ½ hour
Tuesday	A ½ to ¾ hour
Wednesday	B 20 to 30 minutes
Thursday	A ½ to ¾ hour
Friday	B 20 to 30 minutes
Saturday	DE ¼ to ½ hour
Sunday	A ½ to one hour

For four weeks:

Monday	DE $\frac{1}{4}$ to $\frac{1}{2}$ hour
Tuesday	B $\frac{1}{2}$ to $\frac{3}{4}$ hour
Wednesday	F 100 m x 6-8
Thursday	B $\frac{1}{2}$ to $\frac{3}{4}$ hour
Friday	DE $\frac{1}{4}$ to $\frac{1}{2}$ hour
Saturday	F 100 m x 6-8
Sunday	W $\frac{1}{2}$ to $\frac{3}{4}$ hour

For four weeks:

Monday	K 200 m x 6-10
Tuesday	GSX x 8
Wednesday	B $\frac{1}{2}$ to $\frac{3}{4}$ hour
Thursday	K 150 m x 6-10
Friday	GSX x 8
Saturday	N 300 m x 4
Sunday	W $\frac{1}{2}$ to one hour

For two weeks:

Monday	300 m x 2 (15 minutes interval)
Tuesday	GSX x 8
Wednesday	L 100 m, 300 m, 600 m
Thursday	B $\frac{1}{2}$ hour
Friday	O 100 m x 6
Saturday	L 800 m x 2
Sunday	W $\frac{1}{2}$ to one hour

For two weeks:

Monday	J x 6-8
Tuesday	GSX x 6
Wednesday	Race 100 m and 400 m
Thursday	B $\frac{1}{2}$ hour
Friday	N 200 m x 4
Saturday	Race 200 m and 400 m
Sunday	W $\frac{1}{2}$ hour

For one week:

Monday	H x 8-10
Tuesday	GSX x 6
Wednesday	Race 400 m
Thursday	B $\frac{1}{2}$ hour
Friday	N 300 m x 2
Saturday	Race 100 m and 200 m
Sunday	W $\frac{1}{2}$ hour

For one week:

Monday	H x 6-8
Tuesday	B $\frac{1}{2}$ hour
Wednesday	Race 100 m and 200 m
Thursday	W $\frac{1}{2}$ hour
Friday	W $\frac{1}{4}$ hour or rest
Saturday	First important race
Sunday	W $\frac{1}{2}$ hour

Continuation of racing:

Monday	H x 8-10
Tuesday	GSX x 6-8
Wednesday	Race
Thursday	B $\frac{1}{2}$ hour
Friday	N 200 m x 3
Saturday	Race
Sunday	W $\frac{1}{2}$ to $\frac{3}{4}$ hour

400 metres – men, 16 to 18 years

For as long as possible:

Monday	A $\frac{1}{2}$ to $\frac{3}{4}$ hour
Tuesday	A $\frac{3}{4}$ to one hour
Wednesday	B $\frac{1}{2}$ to $\frac{3}{4}$ hour
Thursday	A $\frac{3}{4}$ to one hour
Friday	N 200 m x 6
Saturday	A $\frac{3}{4}$ to 1 $\frac{1}{4}$ hours
Sunday	B $\frac{1}{2}$ to one hour

For two weeks:

Monday	DE $\frac{1}{2}$ to $\frac{3}{4}$ hour
Tuesday	A $\frac{3}{4}$ to one hour
Wednesday	B $\frac{3}{4}$ to one hour
Thursday	A $\frac{3}{4}$ to one hour
Friday	B $\frac{1}{2}$ hour
Saturday	D and E $\frac{1}{2}$ to $\frac{3}{4}$ hour
Sunday	A $\frac{3}{4}$ to 1 $\frac{1}{4}$ hours

For two weeks:

Monday	DE $\frac{1}{2}$ to $\frac{3}{4}$ hour
Tuesday	B $\frac{3}{4}$ to one hour
Wednesday	F 100 m x 8
Thursday	B $\frac{3}{4}$ to one hour
Friday	DE $\frac{1}{2}$ to $\frac{3}{4}$ hour
Saturday	F 100 m x 8-10
Sunday	W one hour

For four weeks:

Monday	K 200 m x 8-12
Tuesday	GSX x 8-10
Wednesday	B $\frac{3}{4}$ to 1 hour
Thursday	K 400 m x 6-8
Friday	GSX x 8-10
Saturday	N 300 m x 6
Sunday	W one hour

For two weeks:

Monday	300 m x 3 or 500 m x 2
Tuesday	GSX x 10
Wednesday	L 100 m, 300 m, 600 m
Thursday	B $\frac{3}{4}$ hour
Friday	O 120 m x 6
Saturday	L 800 m x 3
Sunday	W one hour

For two weeks:

Monday	J x 8-10
Tuesday	GSX x 8
Wednesday	Race 100 m and 400 m
Thursday	B $\frac{3}{4}$ hour
Friday	N 200 m x 6
Saturday	Race 200 m and 400 m
Sunday	W $\frac{3}{4}$ hour

For one week:

Monday	H x 12
Tuesday	GSX x 8
Wednesday	Race 400 m
Thursday	B $\frac{3}{4}$ hour
Friday	N 300 m x 3
Saturday	Race 100m and 200m
Sunday	W $\frac{3}{4}$ hour

For one week:

Monday	H x 12
Tuesday	B $\frac{1}{2}$ to $\frac{3}{4}$ hour
Wednesday	Race 200 m x 2
Thursday	W $\frac{1}{2}$ to $\frac{3}{4}$ hour
Friday	W $\frac{1}{2}$ hour or rest
Saturday	First important race
Sunday	W $\frac{3}{4}$ hour

Continuation of racing:

Monday	H x 12
Tuesday	GSX x 8
Wednesday	Race
Thursday	B $\frac{1}{2}$ to $\frac{3}{4}$ hour
Friday	N 200 m x 4
Saturday	Race
Sunday	W $\frac{3}{4}$ to one hour

400 metres – men

For as long as possible:

Monday	A $\frac{1}{2}$ hour
Tuesday	A one hour
Wednesday	B $\frac{3}{4}$ to one hour
Thursday	A one hour
Friday	N 200 m x 6
Saturday	A one to 1 $\frac{1}{2}$ hours
Sunday	B $\frac{3}{4}$ to one hour

For two weeks:

Monday	DE $\frac{3}{4}$ hour
Tuesday	A one hour
Wednesday	B one hour
Thursday	A one hour
Friday	B $\frac{3}{4}$ hour
Saturday	DE $\frac{3}{4}$ hour
Sunday	A one to 1 $\frac{1}{2}$ hours

For two weeks:

Monday	DE $\frac{3}{4}$ hour
Tuesday	B one hour
Wednesday	F 100 m x 10
Thursday	B one hour
Friday	D and E $\frac{3}{4}$ hour
Saturday	F 100 m x10
Sunday	W one hour

For four weeks:

Monday	K 200m x 10-12
Tuesday	GS and X x 10
Wednesday	B one hour
Thursday	K 400 m x 6-10
Friday	GS
Saturday	N 300 m x 6
Sunday	W one hour

For two weeks:

Monday	300 m x 3 or 500 m x 2
Tuesday	GSX x 10
Wednesday	100 m, 300 m, 600 m
Thursday	B one hour
Friday	O 120 m x 6
Saturday	L 800 m x 3
Sunday	W one hour

For two weeks:

Monday	J x 10
Tuesday	GSX x 10
Wednesday	Race 100 m and 400 m
Thursday	B one hour
Friday	N 200 m x 6
Saturday	Race 200 m and 400 m
Sunday	W one hour

For one week:

Monday	H x 16
Tuesday	GSX x 10
Wednesday	Race 400 m x 2
Thursday	B one hour
Friday	N 300 m x 3
Saturday	Race 100 m and 200 m
Sunday	W $3/4$ hour

For one week:

Monday	H x 12
Tuesday	B $3/4$ hour
Wednesday	Race 200 m x 2
Thursday	W $3/4$ hour
Friday	W hour or rest
Saturday	First important race
Sunday	W one hour

Continuation of racing:

Monday	H x 12
Tuesday	GSX x 10
Wednesday	Race
Thursday	B $^3/_4$ to one hour
Friday	N 200 m x 4
Saturday	Race
Sunday	W one hour

400 metres – women

For as long as possible:

Monday	A $^1/_2$ hour
Tuesday	A $^3/_4$ hour
Wednesday	B $^1/_2$ to $^3/_4$ hour
Thursday	A $^3/_4$ hour
Friday	N 200 m x 6
Saturday	A $^3/_4$ to 1 1/4 hours
Sunday	B $^1/_2$ to one hour

For two weeks:

Monday	DE $^1/_2$ to $^3/_4$ hour
Tuesday	A $^3/_4$ to one hour
Wednesday	B $^3/_4$ to one hour
Thursday	A $^3/_4$ to one hour
Friday	B $^1/_2$ hour
Saturday	DE $^1/_2$ to $^3/_4$ hour
Sunday	A $^3/_4$ to 1 1/4 hours

For two weeks:

Monday	DE $^1/_2$ to $^3/_4$ hour
Tuesday	B $^3/_4$ to one hour
Wednesday	F 100 m x 8
Thursday	B $^3/_4$ to one hour
Friday	DE $^1/_2$ to $^3/_4$ hour
Saturday	F 100 m x 8-10
Sunday	W one hour

For four weeks:

Monday	K 200 m x 8-12
Tuesday	GSX x 8-10
Wednesday	B ¾ to one hour
Thursday	K 400 m x 6-8
Friday	GSX x 8-10
Saturday	N 300 m x 6
Sunday	W one hour

For two weeks:

Monday	300 m x 3 or 500 m x 2
Tuesday	GSX x 10
Wednesday	100 m, 300 m, 600 m
Thursday	B ¾ hour
Friday	O 120 m x 6
Saturday	L 800 m x 3
Sunday	W one hour

For two weeks:

Monday	J x 8-10
Tuesday	GSX x 8
Wednesday	Race 100 m and 400 m
Thursday	B ¾ hour
Friday	N 200 m x 6
Saturday	Race 200 m and 400 m
Sunday	W ¾ hour

For one week:

Monday	H x 12
Tuesday	GSX x 8
Wednesday	Race 400 m
Thursday	B ¾ hour
Friday	N 300 m x 3
Saturday	Race 100 m and 200 m
Sunday	W ¾ hour

For one week:

Monday	H x 12
Tuesday	B$\frac{1}{2}$ to $\frac{3}{4}$ hour
Wednesday	Race 200 m x 2
Thursday	W $\frac{1}{2}$ to $\frac{3}{4}$ hour
Friday	W $\frac{1}{2}$ hour or rest
Saturday	First important race
Sunday	W $\frac{3}{4}$ hour

Continuation of racing:

Monday	H x 12
Tuesday	GSX x 8
Wednesday	Race
Thursday	B 1/2 to $\frac{3}{4}$ hour
Friday	N 200 m x 4
Saturday	Race
Sunday	W $\frac{3}{4}$ to one hour

Middle and distance track
Middle distance track – boys, 13 to 14 years

For as long as possible:

Monday	A $\frac{1}{2}$ to $\frac{3}{4}$ hour
Tuesday	A $\frac{3}{4}$ to 1 $\frac{1}{4}$ hour
Wednesday	L 3,000 m
Thursday	A $\frac{1}{4}$ to 1 $\frac{1}{4}$ hours
Friday	B $\frac{1}{2}$ hour
Saturday	L 5,000m
Sunday	A $\frac{3}{4}$ to 1 $\frac{1}{2}$ hours

For four weeks:

Monday	F 80 m x 6-8
Tuesday	A $\frac{3}{4}$ to 1 $\frac{1}{4}$ hours
Wednesday	D and E $\frac{1}{2}$ hour
Thursday	B $\frac{1}{2}$ to $\frac{3}{4}$ hour
Friday	F 80 m x 6-8
Saturday	D and E $\frac{1}{2}$ hour
Sunday	A $\frac{3}{4}$ to 1 $\frac{1}{4}$ hours

For four weeks:

Monday	K 200 m x 6-10
Tuesday	PQR 80 m x 2 and O 80 m x 2
Wednesday	B $\frac{1}{2}$ to $\frac{3}{4}$ hour
Thursday	K 200 m x 6-10
Friday	F 80 m x 4-6
Saturday	L 3,000 m
Sunday	A $\frac{3}{4}$ to 1 $\frac{1}{4}$ hours

For four weeks:

Monday	J x 6-8
Tuesday	B $\frac{1}{2}$ to $\frac{3}{4}$ hour
Wednesday	L 200 m and 600 m
Thursday	A $\frac{1}{2}$ hour
Friday	O 80 m x 3
Saturday	Race 800 m or 1,500 m
Sunday	W $\frac{1}{4}$ to 1 hour

For one week:

Monday	H x 8-10
Tuesday	B $\frac{1}{2}$ hour
Wednesday	L race distance, M fast
Thursday	B $\frac{1}{2}$ to $\frac{3}{4}$ hour
Friday	N 200 m x 3
Saturday	Race 400 m or 800 m
Sunday	W $\frac{3}{4}$ to one hour

For one week:

Monday	H x 8
Tuesday	B $\frac{1}{2}$ hour
Wednesday	L 200 m
Thursday	W $\frac{1}{2}$ hour
Friday	W $\frac{1}{2}$ hour or rest
Saturday	First important race
Sunday	W $\frac{3}{4}$ to one hour

Continuation of racing:

Monday	B $\frac{1}{2}$ hour
Tuesday	N 100 m x 3
Wednesday	Race or L 400 m
Thursday	B $\frac{1}{2}$ hour
Friday	N 100 m x 43
Saturday	Race or L 400 m or 800 m
Sunday	W $\frac{3}{4}$ to one hour

Middle distance track – boys 15 to 16 years

For as long as possible:

Monday	B $\frac{1}{2}$ to $\frac{3}{4}$ hour
Tuesday	A one to 1 $\frac{1}{4}$ hours
Wednesday	L 3000 m
Thursday	A one to 1 $\frac{1}{4}$ hours
Friday	B $\frac{1}{2}$ hour
Saturday	L 5,000 m
Sunday	A one to 1 $\frac{1}{2}$ hours

For four weeks:

Monday	F 100 m x 6-8
Tuesday	A one to 1 $\frac{1}{4}$ hours
Wednesday	D and E $\frac{1}{2}$ to $\frac{3}{4}$ hour
Thursday	B $\frac{1}{2}$ to $\frac{3}{4}$ hour
Friday	F 100 m x 6-8
Saturday	D and E 1/2 to $\frac{3}{4}$ hour
Sunday	A one to 1 $\frac{1}{2}$ hours

For four weeks:

Monday	K 400 m x 8-12
Tuesday	PQR 100 m x 2 and O 100 m x 2
Wednesday	B $\frac{1}{2}$ to $\frac{3}{4}$ hour
Thursday	K 200 m x 8-12
Friday	F 100 m x 6
Saturday	L 3,000 m
Sunday	A one to 1 $\frac{1}{2}$ hours

For four weeks:

Monday	J x 6-8
Tuesday	B $\frac{1}{2}$ to $\frac{3}{4}$ hour
Wednesday	L 200 m and 600 m
Thursday	W $\frac{3}{4}$ hour
Friday	O 100 m x 4
Saturday	Race 800 m or 1,500 m
Sunday	W one to 1 $\frac{1}{2}$ hours

For one week:

Monday	H x 12
Tuesday	B $\frac{1}{2}$ hour
Wednesday	L race distance
Thursday	B $\frac{1}{2}$ hour
Friday	N 200 m x 4
Saturday	Race 400 m or 800 m
Sunday	W one hour

For one week:

Monday	H x 8-12
Tuesday	B $1/2$ hour
Wednesday	L 100 m and 400 m
Thursday	W $3/4$ hour
Friday	W $1/2$ hour
Saturday	First important race
Sunday	W one hour or more

Continuation of racing:

Monday	B $1/2$ hour
Tuesday	N 200 m x 4
Wednesday	Race or L
Thursday	B $1/2$ hour
Friday	N 200 m x 4
Saturday	Race or L
Sunday	W one hour or more

Middle distance track – men, 17 to 18 years

For as long as possible:

Monday	B $3/4$ hour
Tuesday	A 1 to 1 $1/4$ hours
Wednesday	L 3,000 m
Thursday	A 1 to 1 $1/4$ hours
Friday	B $1/2$ hour
Saturday	L 5,000 m
Sunday	A 1 $1/2$ hours or more

For four weeks:

Monday	F 100 m x 8-10
Tuesday	A 1 to 1 $1/2$ hours
Wednesday	D and E $3/4$ hour
Thursday	B $3/4$ hour
Friday	F 100 m x 8-10
Saturday	D and E $3/4$ hour
Sunday	A 1 $1/2$ hours or more

For four weeks:

Monday	K 400 m x 10-15
Tuesday	PQR 100 m x 2 and O 100 m x 4
Wednesday	B $\frac{3}{4}$ hour
Thursday	K 200 m x 12-16
Friday	F 100 m x 6-8
Saturday	L 3,000 m
Sunday	A 1 $\frac{1}{2}$ hours or more

For four weeks:

Monday	J x 8-10
Tuesday	B $\frac{3}{4}$ hour
Wednesday	L 200 m and 600 m
Thursday	W $\frac{3}{4}$ hour
Friday	O 100 m x 6
Saturday	Race 800 m or 1,500 m
Sunday	W one to 1 $\frac{1}{4}$ hours

For one week:

Monday	H x 16
Tuesday	B $\frac{1}{2}$ hour
Wednesday	L race distance
Thursday	B $\frac{3}{4}$ hour
Friday	N 200 m x 4
Saturday	Race 400 m or 800 m
Sunday	W one hour

For one week:

Monday	H x 12
Tuesday	B $\frac{1}{2}$ hour
Wednesday	L 100 m and 400 m
Thursday	W $\frac{3}{4}$ hour
Friday	W $\frac{1}{2}$ hour
Saturday	First important race
Sunday	W one hour or more

Continuation of racing:

Monday	B $\frac{3}{4}$ hour
Tuesday	N 200 m x 4
Wednesday	Race or L
Thursday	B $\frac{3}{4}$ hour
Friday	N 200 m x 4
Saturday	Race or L
Sunday	W one hour or more

Middle distance track – men, 19 to 20 years

For as long as possible:

Monday	B $\frac{3}{4}$ to one hour
Tuesday	A one to 1 $\frac{1}{2}$ hours
Wednesday	L 5,000 m
Thursday	A one to 1 $\frac{1}{2}$ hours
Friday	B $\frac{3}{4}$ hour
Saturday	L 10,000 m
Sunday	A 1 $\frac{1}{2}$ to two hours

For four weeks:

Monday	F 100 m x 10
Tuesday	A one to 1 $\frac{1}{2}$ hours
Wednesday	D and E $\frac{3}{4}$ to one hour
Thursday	B $\frac{3}{4}$ to one hour
Friday	F 100 m x 10
Saturday	D and E $\frac{3}{4}$ to one hour
Sunday	A 1 $\frac{1}{2}$ to two hours

For four weeks:

Monday	K 400 m x 12-16
Tuesday	PQR 100 m x 2 and O 100 m x 4
Wednesday	B $\frac{3}{4}$ to one hour
Thursday	K 200 m x 15-20
Friday	F 100 m x 8
Saturday	L 3,000 m or 5,000 m
Sunday	A 1 $\frac{1}{2}$ to two hours

For four weeks:

Monday	J x 10-12
Tuesday	B $\frac{3}{4}$ to one hour
Wednesday	L 200 m and 600 m
Thursday	W $\frac{3}{4}$ hour
Friday	O 100 m x 6
Saturday	Race 800 m or 1,500 m
Sunday	W 1 $\frac{1}{2}$ hours

For one week:

Monday	H x 16
Tuesday	B $\frac{3}{4}$ hour
Wednesday	L race distance
Thursday	B $\frac{3}{4}$ hour
Friday	N 200 m x 4
Saturday	Race 400 m or 800 m
Sunday	W 1 $\frac{1}{2}$ hours

For one week:

Monday	H x 12
Tuesday	B $\frac{1}{2}$ hour
Wednesday	L 100 m and 400 m
Thursday	W $\frac{3}{4}$ hour
Friday	W $\frac{1}{2}$ hour
Saturday	First important race
Sunday	W 1 $\frac{1}{2}$ hours

Continuation of racing:

Monday	B $\frac{3}{4}$ hour
Tuesday	N 200 m x 4
Wednesday	Race or L
Thursday	B $\frac{3}{4}$ hour
Friday	N 200 m x 4
Saturday	Race or L
Sunday	W 1 $\frac{1}{2}$ hours

Middle distance track – men

For as long as possible:

Monday	B one hour
Tuesday	A 1 $\frac{1}{2}$ hours
Wednesday	L 5,000 m
Thursday	A 1 $\frac{1}{2}$ hours
Friday	B $\frac{3}{4}$ hour and hills
Saturday	L 10,000 m
Sunday	A 1 $\frac{1}{2}$ hours or more

For four weeks:

Monday	F 120 m x 10
Tuesday	A 1 $\frac{1}{2}$ hours
Wednesday	D and E one hour
Thursday	B one hour
Friday	F 120 m x 10
Saturday	D and E 1 hour
Sunday	A 1 $\frac{1}{2}$ hours or more

For four weeks:

Monday	K 400 m x 15-20
Tuesday	PQR 100 m x 2 and O 100 m x 4
Wednesday	B one hour
Thursday	K 200 m x 15-20
Friday	F 100 m x 10
Saturday	L 3,000 m or 5,000 m
Sunday	A 1 $\frac{1}{2}$ hours or more

For four weeks:

Monday	J x 12-14
Tuesday	B one hour
Wednesday	L 200 m and 600 m
Thursday	A one hour
Friday	O 100m x 6
Saturday	Race 800 m or 1,500 m
Sunday	W 1 $\frac{1}{2}$ hours

For one week:

Monday	H x 20
Tuesday	B one hour
Wednesday	L race distance
Thursday	B $3/4$ hour
Friday	N 200 m x 6
Saturday	Race 400 m or 800 m
Sunday	W 1 $1/2$ hours

For one week:

Monday	H x 16
Tuesday	B $3/4$ hour
Wednesday	L 100 m and 400 m
Thursday	W $3/4$ hour
Friday	W $1/2$ hour
Saturday	First important race
Sunday	W 1 $1/2$ hours

Continuation of racing:

Monday	B one hour
Tuesday	N 200 m x 6
Wednesday	Race or J x 12
Thursday	B one hour
Friday	N 200 m x 6
Saturday	Race or L
Sunday	W 1 $1/2$ hours

3,000 metres – boys, 15 and 16 years

For as long as possible:

Monday	A one hour
Tuesday	A one to 1 $1/2$ hours
Wednesday	L 5,000 m
Thursday	A one to 1 $1/2$ hours
Friday	B $1/2$ to $3/4$ hour
Saturday	L 10,000 m
Sunday	A 1 $1/4$ to 1 $1/2$ hours

For four weeks:

Monday	D and E $\frac{3}{4}$ hour
Tuesday	A one to 1 $\frac{1}{2}$ hours
Wednesday	B $\frac{3}{4}$ hour
Thursday	B and E $\frac{3}{4}$ hour
Friday	F 100 m x 8-10
Saturday	L 5,000 m
Sunday	A 1 $\frac{1}{2}$ to two hours

For four weeks:

Monday	L 3,000 m
Tuesday	K 400 m x 8-12
Wednesday	A one to 1 $\frac{1}{2}$ hours
Thursday	K 200 m x 10-16
Friday	F 100 m x 8-10
Saturday	L 5,000 m
Sunday	A one to 1 $\frac{1}{2}$ hours

For four weeks:

Monday	J x 6-10
Tuesday	B $\frac{3}{4}$ hour
Wednesday	L 200 m and MD
Thursday	W one hour
Friday	N 300 m x 3
Saturday	Race 1,500 m or 3,000 m
Sunday	W one to 1 $\frac{1}{2}$ hours

For one week:

Monday	H x 12-16
Tuesday	W $\frac{3}{4}$ hour
Wednesday	L 3,000 m fast
Thursday	B $\frac{3}{4}$ hour
Friday	N 200 m x 3
Saturday	Race 3,000 m
Sunday	W one hour

For one week:

Monday	H x 12
Tuesday	B $\frac{3}{4}$ hour
Wednesday	L 800 m
Thursday	W $\frac{3}{4}$ hour
Friday	W $\frac{1}{2}$ hour
Saturday	First important race
Sunday	W one to 1 $\frac{1}{2}$ hours

Continuation of racing:

Monday	B $\frac{3}{4}$ hour
Tuesday	N 200 m x 4
Wednesday	Race 200 m and MD
Thursday	B $\frac{3}{4}$ hour
Friday	W $\frac{1}{2}$ hour
Saturday	Race or L
Sunday	W one to 1 $\frac{1}{2}$ hours

Distance track – men, 17 to 18 years

For as long as possible:

Monday	B $\frac{3}{4}$ to one hour
Tuesday	A one to 1 $\frac{1}{2}$ hours
Wednesday	L 5,000 m
Thursday	A one to 1 $\frac{1}{2}$ hours
Friday	B $\frac{3}{4}$ to one hour
Saturday	L 10,000 m
Sunday	A 1 $\frac{1}{2}$ hours or more

For four weeks:

Monday	F 100 m x 8-10
Tuesday	A one to 1 $\frac{1}{2}$ hours
Wednesday	D and E $\frac{3}{4}$ hour
Thursday	A one to $\frac{1}{2}$ hours
Friday	F 100 m x 8-10
Saturday	D and E $\frac{3}{4}$ hour
Sunday	A 1 $\frac{1}{2}$ hours or more

For four weeks:

Monday	K 400 m x 10-15
Tuesday	A one to 1 $\frac{1}{2}$ hours
Wednesday	B $\frac{3}{4}$ hour
Thursday	K 200 m x 12-16
Friday	F 100 m x 6-8
Saturday	L 5,000 m
Sunday	A 1 $\frac{1}{2}$ hours or more

For four weeks:

Monday	J x 8-10
Tuesday	A one to 1 $\frac{1}{2}$ hours
Wednesday	L 200 m and 800 m or 1,500 m
Thursday	B $\frac{3}{4}$ hour
Friday	0 100 m x 4
Saturday	Race 3,000 m or 1,500 m
Sunday	W one hour or more

For one week:

Monday	H x 16
Tuesday	B $\frac{3}{4}$ hour
Wednesday	L race distance
Thursday	B $\frac{1}{2}$ hour
Friday	N 200 m x 4
Saturday	Race 1,500 m
Sunday	A one hour

For one week:

Monday	H x 12-16
Tuesday	B $\frac{1}{2}$ hour
Wednesday	L 800 m
Thursday	W $\frac{1}{2}$ hour
Friday	W $\frac{1}{2}$ hour
Saturday	First important race
Sunday	W one to 1 $\frac{1}{2}$ hours

Continuation of racing:

Monday	B ³⁄₄ hour
Tuesday	N 200 m x 4
Wednesday	Race or L
Thursday	B ³⁄₄ hour
Friday	N 200 m x 4
Saturday	Race or L
Sunday	W one to 1 ¹⁄₂ hours

Distance track – men, 19 to 20 years

For as long as possible:

Monday	B ³⁄₄ to one hour
Tuesday	A 1 ¹⁄₂ hours
Wednesday	L 5,000 m
Thursday	A 1 ¹⁄₂ hours
Friday	B ³⁄₄ hour
Saturday	L 10,000 m
Sunday	A two hours

For four weeks:

Monday	F 100 m x 10
Tuesday	A 1 ¹⁄₂ hours
Wednesday	D and E ³⁄₄ to one hour
Thursday	A 1 ¹⁄₂ hours
Friday	F 100 m x 10
Saturday	DE ³⁄₄ to one hour
Sunday	A two hours

For four weeks:

Monday	K 400 m x 12-16
Tuesday	A 1 ¹⁄₂ hours
Wednesday	B ³⁄₄ to one hour
Thursday	K 200 m x 15-20
Friday	F 100 m x 8
Saturday	L 5,000 m
Sunday	A two hours

For four weeks:

Monday	J x 10-12
Tuesday	A 1 $\frac{1}{2}$ hours
Wednesday	L 200 m and 800 m or 1,500 m
Thursday	B $\frac{3}{4}$ hour
Friday	O 100 m x 4
Saturday	Race 3,000 m or 5,000 m
Sunday	W 1 $\frac{1}{2}$ hours

For one week:

Monday	H x 16-20
Tuesday	B $\frac{3}{4}$ hour
Wednesday	L race distance
Thursday	B $\frac{3}{4}$ hour
Friday	N 200 m x 4
Saturday	Race 1,500 m
Sunday	W 1 $\frac{1}{2}$ hours

For one week:

Monday	H x 12-16
Tuesday	B $\frac{3}{4}$ hour
Wednesday	L 800 m
Thursday	W $\frac{3}{4}$ hour
Friday	W $\frac{1}{2}$ hour
Saturday	First important race
Sunday	W 1 $\frac{1}{2}$ hours

Continuation of racing:

Monday	B one hour
Tuesday	N 200 m x 4
Wednesday	Race or L
Thursday	B $\frac{3}{4}$ hour
Friday	N 200 m x 4
Saturday	Race or L
Sunday	W 1 $\frac{1}{2}$ hours or more

Distance track – men, senior

For as long as possible:

Monday	B one hour
Tuesday	A 1 $\frac{1}{2}$ hours
Wednesday	L 10,000 m
Thursday	A 1 $\frac{1}{2}$ hours
Friday	B one hour
Saturday	L 10,000 m
Sunday	A two hours or more

For four weeks:

Monday	F 120 m x 10
Tuesday	A 1 $\frac{1}{2}$ hours
Wednesday	D and E one hour
Thursday	A 1 $\frac{1}{2}$ hours
Friday	F 120 m x 10
Saturday	D and E one hour
Sunday	A two hours or more

For four weeks:

Monday	K 400 m x 15-20
Tuesday	A 1 $\frac{1}{2}$ hours
Wednesday	B one hour
Thursday	K 200 m x 15-20
Friday	F 100 m x 10
Saturday	L 5,000 m or 10,000 m
Sunday	A two hours or more

For four weeks:

Monday	J x 12-14
Tuesday	A 1 $\frac{1}{2}$ hours
Wednesday	L 200 m and 800 m or 1,500 m
Thursday	B one hour
Friday	0 100 m x 6
Saturday	Race 3,000 m, 5,000 m or 10,000 m
Sunday	W 1 $\frac{1}{2}$ to two hours

For one week:

Monday	H x 20
Tuesday	B one hour
Wednesday	L race distance
Thursday	B ¾ hour
Friday	N 200 m x 6
Saturday	Race 1,500 m
Sunday	W 1 ½ hours

For one week:

Monday	H x 16
Tuesday	B ¾ hour
Wednesday	L 800 m
Thursday	W ¾ hour
Friday	W ½ hour
Saturday	First important race
Sunday	W 1 ½ hours

Continuation of racing:

Monday	B one hour
Tuesday	N 200 m x 6
Wednesday	Race or L 3,000 m
Thursday	B one hour
Friday	N 200 m x 6
Saturday	Race or L 5,000 m
Sunday	W 1 ½ hours or more

Middle distance track – girls and boys, 10 to 12 years

For as long as possible:

Monday	A ¼ to ½ hour
Tuesday	A ¼ to ¾ hour
Wednesday	L 2,000 m
Thursday	A 1/2 to ¾ hour
Friday	B ¼ to ½ hour
Saturday	L 3,000 m
Sunday	A ½ to one hour

For four weeks:

Monday	F 60 m x 6
Tuesday	A $\frac{1}{4}$ to $\frac{3}{4}$ hour
Wednesday	D and E $\frac{1}{4}$ to $\frac{1}{2}$ hour
Thursday	B $\frac{1}{4}$ to $\frac{1}{2}$ hour
Friday	F 60 m x 6
Saturday	D and E $\frac{1}{4}$ to $\frac{1}{2}$ hour
Sunday	A $\frac{1}{2}$ to one hour

For four weeks:

Monday	J x 4-6
Tuesday	PQR 60 m x 2
Wednesday	B $\frac{1}{4}$ to $\frac{1}{2}$ hour
Thursday	K 150 m x 2-4
Friday	F 60 m x 4-6
Saturday	L 1,600 m
Sunday	A $\frac{1}{2}$ to one hour

For four weeks:

Monday	H x 4-8
Tuesday	B $\frac{1}{4}$ to $\frac{1}{2}$ hour
Wednesday	L 100 m and 400 m
Thursday	A $\frac{1}{4}$ to $\frac{1}{2}$ hour
Friday	Rest
Saturday	Race 400 m or 800 m
Sunday	W $\frac{1}{2}$ to $\frac{3}{4}$ hour

For one week:

Monday	MH 4-8
Tuesday	B $\frac{1}{4}$ hour
Wednesday	L race distance
Thursday	B $\frac{1}{4}$ hour
Friday	Rest
Saturday	Race 200 m or 400 m
Sunday	W $\frac{1}{2}$ to one hour

For one week:

Monday	H 4-8
Tuesday	B $\frac{1}{4}$ hour
Wednesday	L 200 m
Thursday	W $\frac{1}{4}$ to $\frac{1}{2}$ hour
Friday	Rest
Saturday	First important race
Sunday	W $\frac{1}{2}$ to one hour

Continuation of racing:

Monday	B $\frac{1}{4}$ to $\frac{1}{2}$ hour
Tuesday	N 100 m x 2
Wednesday	Race or L 200 m
Thursday	B $\frac{1}{4}$ hour
Friday	Rest
Saturday	Race or L 400 m or 800 m
Sunday	W $\frac{1}{2}$ to one hour

Middle distance track – girls, 13 to 14 years

For as long as possible:

Monday	B $\frac{1}{2}$ to $\frac{3}{4}$ hour
Tuesday	A $\frac{1}{2}$ to one hour
Wednesday	L 2,400 m
Thursday	A $\frac{1}{2}$ to one hour
Friday	B $\frac{1}{2}$ to $\frac{3}{4}$ hour
Saturday	L 4,000 m
Sunday	A $\frac{3}{4}$ to 1 $\frac{1}{4}$ hours

For four weeks:

Monday	F 80 m x 6-8
Tuesday	A $\frac{1}{2}$ to one hour
Wednesday	DE 20 to 30 minutes
Thursday	B $\frac{1}{2}$ to $\frac{3}{4}$ hour
Friday	F 80 m x 6-8
Saturday	DE 20 to 30 minutes
Sunday	A $\frac{3}{4}$ to 1 $\frac{1}{4}$ hours

For four weeks:

Monday	K 200 m x 4-6
Tuesday	PQR 80 m x 2 and O 100 m x 2
Wednesday	B $\frac{1}{2}$ to $\frac{3}{4}$ hour
Thursday	K 200 m x 4-6
Friday	F 80 m x 4-6
Saturday	L 2,000 m
Sunday	A $\frac{3}{4}$ to 1 $\frac{1}{4}$ hours

For four weeks:

Monday	H x 8-12
Tuesday	B $\frac{1}{2}$ to $\frac{3}{4}$ hour
Wednesday	L 100 m and 400 m
Thursday	A $\frac{1}{2}$ hour
Friday	N 100 m x 3
Saturday	Race 400 m or 800 m
Sunday	W $\frac{1}{2}$ to one hour

For one week:

Monday	H x 8
Tuesday	B 20 to 30 minutes
Wednesday	L race distance
Thursda	B 20 to 30 minutes
Friday	N 100 m x 3
Saturda	Race 200 m or 400 m
Sunday	W $\frac{3}{4}$ to one hour

For one week:

Monday	H x 6-8
Tuesday	B 20 to 30 minutes
Wednesday	L 200 m
Thursday	W $\frac{1}{2}$ hour
Friday	W $\frac{1}{2}$ or rest
Saturda	First important race
Sunday	W $\frac{3}{4}$ to one hour

Continuation of racing:

Monday	B 20 to 30 minutes
Tuesday	N 100 m x 3
Wednesday	Race or L 400 m
Thursday	B 20 to 30 minutes
Friday	N 100 m x 3
Saturday	Race or L 400 m or 800 m
Sunday	W $\frac{1}{2}$ to $\frac{3}{4}$ hour

Middle distance track – women, 15 to 17 years

For as long as possible:

Monday	B $\frac{3}{4}$ to one hour
Tuesday	A $\frac{3}{4}$ to 1 $\frac{1}{4}$ hours
Wednesday	L 3,000 m
Thursday	A $\frac{3}{4}$ to 1 $\frac{1}{4}$ hours
Friday	B $\frac{1}{2}$ to $\frac{3}{4}$ hour (hills)
Saturday	L 5,000 m
Sunday	A one to 1 $\frac{1}{2}$ hours

For four weeks:

Monday	F 100 m x 8-10
Tuesday	A $\frac{3}{4}$ to 1 $\frac{1}{4}$ hours
Wednesday	D and E $\frac{1}{2}$ to $\frac{3}{4}$ hour
Thursday	B $\frac{3}{4}$ to 1 one hour
Friday	F 100 m x 8-10
Saturday	D and E $\frac{1}{2}$ to $\frac{3}{4}$ hour
Sunday	A one to 1 $\frac{1}{2}$ hours

For four weeks:

Monday	K 200 m x 8-12
Tuesday	PQR 100 m x 2 and O 100 m x 3
Wednesday	B $\frac{3}{4}$ to one hour
Thursday	K 200 m x 8-12
Friday	F 100 m x 6
Saturday	L 3,000 m
Sunday	A one to 1 $\frac{1}{2}$ hours

For four weeks:

Monday	J x 8-10
Tuesday	B ¾ to one hour
Wednesday	L 200 m and 600 m
Thursday	A ¾ hour
Friday	O 100 m x 4
Saturday	Race 800 m or 1,500 m
Sunday	W ¾ to 1 ¼ hours

For one week:

Monday	H x 8-12
Tuesday	B ½ to ¾ hour
Wednesday	L race distance
Thursday	B ½ to ¾ hour
Friday	N 200 m x 4
Saturday	Race 400 m or 800 m
Sunday	W ¾ to one hour

For one week:

Monday	H x 8-12
Tuesday	B ½ hour
Wednesday	L 100 m and 400 m
Thursday	W ½ hour
Friday	W ½ hour
Saturday	First important race
Sunday	W ¾ to 1 ¼ hours

Continuation of racing:

Monday	B ½ to ¾ hour
Tuesday	N 200 m x 4
Wednesday	Race or J x 8
Thursday	B ½ to ¾ hour
Friday	N 200 m x 4
Saturday	Race or L 800 m or 1,500 m
Sunday	W ¾ to one hour

Middle distance track – women

For as long as possible:

Monday	B $\frac{3}{4}$ to one hour
Tuesday	A one to 1 $\frac{1}{2}$ hours
Wednesday	L 3,000 m
Thursday	A one to 1 $\frac{1}{2}$ hours
Friday	B $\frac{3}{4}$ hour
Saturday	L 5,000 m
Sunday	A 1 $\frac{1}{2}$ hours or more

For four weeks:

Monday	F 100 m x 10
Tuesday	A one to 1 $\frac{1}{2}$ hours
Wednesday	D and E $\frac{3}{4}$ to one hour
Thursday	B $\frac{3}{4}$ to 1 hour
Friday	F 100 m x 10
Saturday	D and E $\frac{3}{4}$ to one hour
Sunday	A 1 $\frac{1}{2}$ hours or more

For four weeks:

Monday	K 400 m x 10-15
Tuesday	PQR 100 m x 2 and O 100 m x 4
Wednesday	B $\frac{3}{4}$ to one hour
Thursday	K 200 m x 12-18
Friday	F 100 m x 8
Saturday	L 3,000 m
Sunday	A 1 $\frac{1}{2}$ hours or more

For four weeks:

Monday	J x 8-10
Tuesday	B $\frac{3}{4}$ to one hour
Wednesday	L 200 m and 600 m
Thursday	A $\frac{3}{4}$ hour
Friday	O 100 m x 6
Saturday	Race 800 m or 1,500 m
Sunday	W one to 1 $\frac{1}{2}$ hours

For one week:

Monday	H x 12-16
Tuesday	B $\frac{3}{4}$ hour
Wednesday	L race distance
Thursday	B $\frac{3}{4}$ hour
Friday	N 200 m x 4
Saturday	Race 400 m or 800 m
Sunday	W one to 1 $\frac{1}{2}$ hours

For one week:

Monday	H x 12
Tuesday	B $\frac{3}{4}$ hour
Wednesday	L 100 m and 400 m
Thursday	W $\frac{3}{4}$ hour
Friday	W $\frac{1}{2}$ hour
Saturday	First important race
Sunday	W one hour or more

Continuation of racing:

Monday	B $\frac{3}{4}$ hour
Tuesday	N 200 m x 4
Wednesday	Race or L
Thursday	B $\frac{3}{4}$ hour
Friday	N 200 m x 4
Saturday	Race or L
Sunday	W one hour or more

3,000 metres track – women, 15 to 17 years

For as long as possible:

Monday	B $\frac{1}{2}$ to $\frac{3}{4}$ hour
Tuesday	A one to 1 $\frac{1}{4}$ hours
Wednesday	L 5,000 m
Thursday	A one to 1 $\frac{1}{4}$ hours
Friday	B $\frac{1}{2}$ hour
Saturday	L 5,000 m
Sunday	A 1 $\frac{1}{4}$ hours or more

For four weeks:

Monday	D and E $\frac{1}{2}$ to $\frac{3}{4}$ hour
Tuesday	A one to 1 $\frac{1}{4}$ hours
Wednesday	B $\frac{1}{2}$ to $\frac{3}{4}$ hour
Thursday	D and E $\frac{1}{2}$ to $\frac{3}{4}$ hour
Friday	F 100 m x 6-8
Saturday	L 5,000 m
Sunday	A 1 $\frac{1}{2}$ hours or more

For four weeks:

Monday	L 3,000 m
Tuesday	K 400 m x 8-12
Wednesday	A one to 1 $\frac{1}{4}$ hours
Thursday	K 200 m x 10-16
Friday	F 100 m x 6- 8
Saturday	L 5,000 m
Sunday	A 1 $\frac{1}{2}$ hours or more

For four weeks:

Monday	J x 6-8
Tuesday	B $\frac{1}{2}$ to $\frac{3}{4}$ hour
Wednesday	L 200 m and middle distance
Thursday	W one hour
Friday	N 300 m x 3
Saturday	Race 1,500 m or 3,000 m
Sunday	A one hour or more

For one week:

Monday	H x 12-16
Tuesday	B $\frac{3}{4}$ hour
Wednesday	L 3,000 m fast
Thursday	B $\frac{1}{2}$ hour
Friday	N 200 m x 3
Saturday	Race 1,500 m
Sunday	W one hour

For one week:

Monday	H x 12
Tuesday	B $\frac{1}{2}$ hour
Wednesday	L 800 m
Thursday	W $\frac{1}{2}$ hour
Friday	W $\frac{1}{2}$ hour
Saturday	First important race
Sunday	W one hour or more

Continuation of racing:

Monday	B $\frac{1}{2}$ to $\frac{3}{4}$ hour
Tuesday	N 200 m x 4
Wednesday	Race 200 m or middle distance
Thursday	B $\frac{1}{2}$ to $\frac{3}{4}$ hour
Friday	W $\frac{1}{2}$ hour
Saturday	Race or L
Sunday	W one hour or more

3,000 metres track – women, senior

For as long as possible:

Monday	B $\frac{3}{4}$ to one hour
Tuesday	A one to 1 $\frac{1}{2}$ hours
Wednesday	L 5,000 m
Thursday	A one to 1 $\frac{1}{2}$ hours
Friday	B $\frac{3}{4}$ hour
Saturday	L 10,000 m
Sunday	A 1 $\frac{1}{2}$ hours or more

For four weeks:

Monday	D and E $\frac{3}{4}$ to one hour
Tuesday	A one to 1 $\frac{1}{2}$ hours
Wednesday	B $\frac{3}{4}$ to one hour
Thursday	D and E $\frac{3}{4}$ to one hour
Friday	F 100 m x 10
Saturday	L 5,000 m
Sunday	A 1 $\frac{1}{2}$ to two hours

For four weeks:

Monday	L 3,000 m
Tuesday	K 400 m x 10-15
Wednesday	A one to 1 $\frac{1}{2}$ hours
Thursday	K 200 m x 12-18
Friday	F 100 m x 10
Saturday	L 5,000 m
Sunday	A 1 $\frac{1}{2}$ hours or more

For four weeks:

Monday	J x 8-10
Tuesday	B $\frac{3}{4}$ to one hour
Wednesday	L 200 m and middle distance
Thursday	W one hour
Friday	N 300 m x 3
Saturday	Race 1,500 m or 3,000 m
Sunday	A 1 $\frac{1}{2}$ hours or more

For one week:

Monday	H x 12-16
Tuesday	B one hour
Wednesday	L 3,000 m
Thursday	B $\frac{1}{2}$ to $\frac{3}{4}$ hour
Friday	N 200 m x 3
Saturday	Race 1,500 m
Sunday	W one hour

For one week:

Monday	H x 12
Tuesday	B $\frac{3}{4}$ hour
Wednesday	L 800 m
Thursday	W $\frac{3}{4}$ hour
Friday	W $\frac{1}{2}$ hour
Saturday	First important race
Sunday	W one to 1 $\frac{1}{2}$ hours

Continuation of racing:

Monday	B $\frac{3}{4}$ hour
Tuesday	N 200 m x 4
Wednesday	Race 200 m or middle distance
Thursday	B $\frac{3}{4}$ hour
Friday	W $\frac{1}{2}$ hour
Saturday	Race or L
Sunday	W one to 1 $\frac{1}{2}$ hours

1,500 metres steeplechase – men, senior

For as long as possible:

Monday	B $\frac{1}{2}$ to $\frac{3}{4}$ hour
Tuesday	A $\frac{3}{4}$ to one hour
Wednesday	L 3,000 m
Thursday	A $\frac{3}{4}$ to one hour
Friday	B $\frac{1}{2}$ to $\frac{3}{4}$ hour (hills)
Saturday	L 5,000 m
Sunday	A one hour or more

For four weeks:

Monday	F 100 m x 8
Tuesday	A one hour
Wednesday	DE $\frac{1}{2}$ to $\frac{3}{4}$ hour
Thursday	B $\frac{3}{4}$ hour
Friday	F 100 m x 8
Saturday	DE $\frac{1}{2}$ to $\frac{3}{4}$ hour
Sunday	A one hour or more

For four weeks:

Monday	K 400 m x 8-12
Tuesday	L 2,000 m and Y $\frac{3}{4}$ effort
Wednesday	B $\frac{3}{4}$ hour
Thursday	K 200 m x 8-12
Friday	PQR 100 m x 2 and O 100 m x 3
Saturda	L 3,000 m or 2,000 m and Y
Sunday	A one hour or more

For four weeks:

Monday	J x 8-10
Tuesday	L 1,500 m and Y $\frac{3}{4}$ effort
Wednesday	L 200 m and 600 m
Thursday	B $\frac{1}{2}$ hour
Friday	YZ $\frac{1}{2}$ hour
Saturday	Race 1,500 m, 800 m or Y 1,500 m
Sunday	W one hour or more

For one week:

Monday	H x 16
Tuesday	B $\frac{1}{2}$ hour
Wednesday	L 1,500 m and Y fast
Thursday	B $\frac{3}{4}$ effort
Friday	N 200m x 3 and YZ
Saturday	Race 800 m
Sunday	W one hour

For one week:

Monday	H x 12
Tuesday	B $\frac{1}{2}$ hour
Wednesday	L 100 m and 400 m
Thursday	Y and W $\frac{1}{2}$ hour
Friday	W $\frac{1}{2}$ hour
Saturday	First important race
Sunday	W one hour

Continuation of racing:

Monday	B $\frac{1}{2}$ hour
Tuesday	N 200 m x 3 and Y
Wednesday	Race or L
Thursday	B $\frac{3}{4}$ hour
Friday	N 200 m x 3 and Y
Saturday	Race or L
Sunday	W one hour or more

2,000 metres steeplechase – men, senior

For as long as possible:

Monday	B $\frac{1}{2}$ to $\frac{3}{4}$ hour
Tuesday	A $\frac{1}{2}$ to 1 $\frac{1}{4}$ hours
Wednesday	L 3,000 m
Thursday	A $\frac{3}{4}$ to 1 $\frac{1}{4}$ hours
Friday	B $\frac{1}{2}$ to $\frac{3}{4}$ hour (hills)
Saturday	L 5,000 m
Sunday	A 1 $\frac{1}{4}$ hours or more

For four weeks:

Monday	F 100 m x 8-10
Tuesday	A $\frac{3}{4}$ to 1 $\frac{1}{4}$ hours
Wednesday	DE $\frac{1}{2}$ to $\frac{3}{4}$ hour
Thursday	B $\frac{3}{4}$ hour
Friday	F 100 m x 8-10
Saturday	DE $\frac{1}{2}$ to $\frac{3}{4}$ hour
Sunday	A 1 $\frac{1}{4}$ hours or more

For four weeks:

Monday	K 400 m x 10-15
Tuesday	L 3,000 m and Y $\frac{3}{4}$ effort
Wednesday	B $\frac{3}{4}$ hour
Thursday	K 200 m x 12-18
Friday	PQR 100 m x 2 and O 100 m x 4
Saturday	L 5,000m or 3,000m YZ
Sunday	A 1 1/2 hours or more

For four weeks:

Monday	J x 8-10
Tuesday	L 2,000 m and Y $\frac{3}{4}$ effort
Wednesday	L 200 m and 800 m
Thursday	B $\frac{3}{4}$ hour
Friday	YZ $\frac{1}{2}$ hour
Saturday	Race 1,500 m, 3,000 m or 2,000 m YZ
Sunday	W one hour or more

For one week:

Monday	H x 16
Tuesday	B ³⁄₄ hour
Wednesday	L 2,000 m Y fast
Thursday	B ¹⁄₂ hour
Friday	N 200 m x 4 and YX
Saturday	Race 800 m or 1,500 m
Sunday	W one hour

For one week:

Monday	H x 12
Tuesday	B ¹⁄₂ hour
Wednesday	L 100 m and 400 m
Thursday	Y and W ¹⁄₂ hour
Friday	W ¹⁄₂ hour
Saturday	First important race
Sunday	W one hour or more

Continuation of racing:

Monday	B ³⁄₄ hour
Tuesday	N 200 m x 4 and YZ
Wednesday	Race or L
Thursday	B ¹⁄₄ hour
Friday	N 200 m x 4 and Y
Saturday	Race or L
Sunday	W one hour or more

3,000 metres steeplechase – men, senior

For as long as possible:

Monday	B one hour
Tuesday	A 1 ¹⁄₂ hours
Wednesday	L 5,000 m
Thursday	A 1 ¹⁄₂ hours
Friday	B ³⁄₄ hour (hills)
Saturday	L 10,000 m
Sunday	A 1 ¹⁄₂ hours or more

For four weeks:

Monday	F 100 m x 10
Tuesday	A 1 $\frac{1}{2}$ hours
Wednesday	DE one hour
Thursday	B one hour
Friday	F 100 m x 10
Saturday	DE one hour
Sunday	A 1 $\frac{1}{2}$ hours or more

For four weeks:

Monday	K 400 m x 15-20
Tuesday	L 3,000 m and Y $\frac{3}{4}$ effort
Wednesday	B one hour
Thursday	K 200 m x 15-20
Friday	PQR 100 m x 2 and O 100 m x 6
Saturday	L 5,000 m or 3,000 m YZ
Sunday	A 1 $\frac{1}{2}$ hours or more

For four weeks:

Monday	J x 10-12
Tuesday	L 2,000 m and Y $\frac{3}{4}$ effort
Wednesday	L 200 m and 800 m
Thursday	B one hour
Friday	YZ $\frac{1}{2}$ hour
Saturday	Race 1,500 m, 3,000 m or 5,000 m
Sunday	W 1 $\frac{1}{2}$ hours

For one week:

Monday	H x 20
Tuesday	B one hour
Wednesday	L 3,000 m Y fast
Thursday	B $\frac{3}{4}$ hour
Friday	N 200 m x 4 and YZ
Saturday	Race 800 m or 1,500 m
Sunday	W 1 to 1 $\frac{1}{2}$ hours

For one week:

Monday	H x 12-16
Tuesday	B $3/4$ hour
Wednesday	L 100 m and 400 m
Thursday	Y and W $1/2$ hour
Friday	W $1/2$ hour
Saturday	First important race
Sunday	W 1 $1/2$ hours

Continuation of racing:

Monday	B $3/4$ hour to one hour
Tuesday	N 200 m x 4 and YZ
Wednesday	Race or L
Thursday	B $3/4$ hour
Friday	N 200 m x 4 and Y
Saturday	Race or L
Sunday	W 1 to 1 $1/2$ hours

Cross-country

There is often a need for cross-country runners to race early in the season in order to support their club teams, so it can become necessary to develop some anaerobic exercise ability while trying to improve your general condition. For this, it is best to use easy fartlek sessions and forms of time trials, which are incorporated into the early conditioning schedule. This is not the best way to train, but it can be essential for cross-country runners.

The fartlek should be of a relatively easy effort with concentration on individual weaknesses. Sessions can include steep hill running with a high knee action, for strengthening the legs generally and the quadriceps and ankles particularly; hill springing for ankle flexibility and power, and striding out downhill or on slopes and across flat areas. Do not overdo the anaerobic sprints so that the session becomes a hard anaerobic workout.

The time trials should be run strongly and evenly in effort on terrain similar to what you will eventually race over; or on a grass track if even-paced running is desired. Do not run at your best effort, but about seven-eighths effort, always knowing you could do a little better and are holding something in reserve.

Use commonsense in applying the schedule. It is only a guide. If your legs feel dead after racing, jog a few days until they have recovered, avoiding speed work. Recovery is important in cross-country because the terrain you race over can pull your legs about.

Control anaerobic training carefully. Practise clearing fences similar to those you experience in racing. This gives full confidence.

Run through soft and sandy ground as often as possible to accustom yourself to relaxing and not driving too hard with the legs. Try to develop a pulling action with the hips held comfortably forward. Cut down your stride length a little. Leg speed should increase.

Jog most mornings as a supplement to your main training sessions and try to incorporate in them a little steep hill running, hill springing and step running. Even fifteen minutes will help to condition your legs and increase your speed later.

Note

A - Long aerobic running

B - Easy fartlek running

C - Strong fartlek running

D - Hill springing

E - Steep hills or step running

F - Leg speed

G - Sprint training

H - 45-metre windsprints every 100 metres

J - 100-metre windsprints every 200 metres

K - Repetitions

L - Time trials

M - Pace judgement running

N - Relaxed striding

O - Fast relaxed running

P - High knee-lift exercise

Q - Long striding exercising

R - Running tall exercising

S - Calisthenics

T - Skipping

U - Cycling

V - Swimming

W - Jogging

X - Sprints starts

Y - Hurdles practice

Z - Water jump practice

Cross-country – boys, under 12

For as long as possible:

Monday	A $\frac{1}{4}$ to $\frac{1}{2}$ hour
Tuesday	B $\frac{1}{4}$ to $\frac{1}{2}$ hour
Wednesday	L 2,000 m
Thursday	A $\frac{1}{4}$ to $\frac{1}{2}$ hour
Friday	W $\frac{1}{4}$ hour or rest
Saturday	L 2,000 m
Sunday	A $\frac{1}{2}$ hour or more

For four weeks:

Monday	B $\frac{1}{4}$ to $\frac{1}{2}$ hour
Tuesday	A $\frac{1}{4}$ to $\frac{1}{2}$ hour
Wednesday	L 2,000 m
Thursday	N 150 m x 4
Friday	W $\frac{1}{4}$ hour or rest
Saturday	L 2,000 m
Sunday	A $\frac{1}{2}$ hour or more

For four weeks:

Monday	H x 6-8
Tuesday	B $\frac{1}{4}$ to $\frac{1}{2}$ hour
Wednesday	L 1,500 m
Thursday	B $\frac{1}{4}$ to $\frac{1}{2}$ hour
Friday	W $\frac{1}{4}$ hour or rest
Saturday	Development races
Sunday	A $\frac{1}{2}$ hour or more

For one week:

Monday	H x 6-8
Tuesday	B $\frac{1}{2}$ hour
Wednesday	L 800 m
Thursday	N 150 m x 4
Friday	Rest
Saturday	Race 2,000 m
Sunday	W $\frac{1}{2}$ to $\frac{3}{4}$ hour

For one week:

Monday	H x 6-8
Tuesday	B $\frac{1}{4}$ to $\frac{1}{2}$ hour
Wednesday	L 800 m
Thursday	W $\frac{1}{2}$ hour
Friday	W $\frac{1}{4}$ hour or rest
Saturday	Race 1,000 m
Sunday	W $\frac{1}{2}$ to $\frac{3}{4}$ hour

For one week:

Monday	H x 6-8
Tuesday	W $\frac{1}{2}$ hour
Wednesday	L 600 m
Thursday	W $\frac{1}{4}$ hour
Friday	Rest
Saturday	First important race
Sunday	W $\frac{1}{2}$ hour or more

Continuation of racing:

Monday	H x 6-8
Tuesday	W $\frac{1}{4}$ to $\frac{1}{2}$ hour
Wednesday	L 800 m
Thursday	B $\frac{1}{4}$ to $\frac{1}{2}$ hour
Friday	W $\frac{1}{4}$ hour or rest
Saturday	Race
Sunday	W $\frac{1}{2}$ hour or more

Cross-country – boys, 12 and 13

For as long as possible:

Monday	A $\frac{1}{2}$ to $\frac{3}{4}$ hour
Tuesday	B $\frac{1}{2}$ hour
Wednesday	L 3,000 m
Thursday	A $\frac{1}{2}$ to $\frac{3}{4}$ hour
Friday	F 80 m x 4-6
Saturday	L 3,000 m
Sunday	A $\frac{3}{4}$ to 1 $\frac{1}{4}$ hours

For four weeks:

Monday	DE $\frac{1}{2}$ hour
Tuesday	A $\frac{1}{2}$ to one hour
Wednesday	L 3,000 m
Thursday	K 200 m x 4-6
Friday	F 80 m x 4-6
Saturday	L 3,000 m
Sunday	A $\frac{3}{4}$ to 1 $\frac{1}{4}$ hours

For four weeks:

Monday	J x 4-6
Tuesday	B $\frac{1}{2}$ to $\frac{3}{4}$ hour
Wednesday	L 3,000 m
Thursday	B $\frac{1}{2}$ hour
Friday	W $\frac{1}{2}$ hour
Saturday	Development races
Sunday	A $\frac{3}{4}$ to 1 $\frac{1}{4}$ hours

For one week:

Monday	H x 8-10
Tuesday	B $\frac{1}{2}$ hour
Wednesday	L 1,000 m
Thursday	N 200 m x 3
Friday	W $\frac{1}{2}$ hour
Saturday	Race 2,500 m
Sunday	W $\frac{3}{4}$ hour

For one week:

Monday	H x 8
Tuesday	B $\frac{1}{2}$ hour
Wednesday	L 800 m
Thursday	B $\frac{1}{2}$ hour
Friday	W $\frac{1}{2}$ hour
Saturday	Race 1,500 m
Sunday	W $\frac{1}{2}$ to $\frac{3}{4}$ hour

For one week:

Monday	H x 8
Tuesday	A $1/2$ hour
Wednesday	L 600 m
Thursday	W $1/2$ hour
Friday	W $1/2$ hour or rest
Saturday	First important race
Sunday	W $3/4$ hour or more

Continuation of racing:

Monday	H x 8
Tuesday	B $1/2$ hour
Wednesday	L 800 m
Thursday	B $1/2$ hour
Friday	W $1/2$ hour
Saturday	Race
Sunday	W $3/4$ hour or more

Cross-country – boys, 14 and 15

For as long as possible:

Monday	B $1/2$ to $3/4$ hour
Tuesday	A $3/4$ to one hour
Wednesday	L 5,000 m
Thursday	A $3/4$ to one hour
Friday	F 100 m x 6
Saturday	L 3,000 m
Sunday	A one hour or more

For four weeks:

Monday	DE $1/2$ to $3/4$ hour
Tuesday	A $3/4$ to one hour
Wednesday	L 3,000 m
Thursday	K 200 m x 6-8
Friday	F 100 m x 6
Saturday	L 3,000 m
Sunday	A one hour or more

For four weeks:

Monday	J x 6-8
Tuesday	B $\frac{1}{2}$ to $\frac{3}{4}$ hour
Wednesday	L 3,000 m
Thursday	B $\frac{1}{2}$ hour
Friday	N 200 m x 4
Saturday	Development races
Sunday	A $\frac{3}{4}$ hour or more

For one week:

Monday	H x 10-12
Tuesday	B $\frac{1}{2}$ hour
Wednesday	L 1,000 m
Thursday	B $\frac{1}{2}$ hour
Friday	W $\frac{1}{2}$ hour
Saturday	Race 3,000 m
Sunday	W $\frac{1}{4}$ hour

For one week:

Monday	H x 8-10
Tuesday	B $\frac{1}{2}$ hour
Wednesday	L 1,000 m
Thursday	B $\frac{1}{2}$ hour
Friday	N 200m x 3
Saturday	Race 2,000 m
Sunday	W $\frac{3}{4}$ hour

For one week:

Monday	H x 8
Tuesday	B $\frac{1}{2}$ hour
Wednesday	L 800 m
Thursday	W $\frac{1}{2}$ hour
Friday	W $\frac{1}{2}$ hour or rest
Saturday	First important race
Sunday	W $\frac{3}{4}$ hour or more

Continuation of racing:

Monday	H x 8-10
Tuesday	B $\frac{1}{2}$ to $\frac{3}{4}$ hour
Wednesday	L 1,000 m
Thursday	B $\frac{1}{2}$ hour
Friday	W $\frac{1}{2}$ hour
Saturday	Race
Sunday	W $\frac{3}{4}$ hour or more

Cross-country – Boys, 16 and 17

For as long as possible:

Monday	B $\frac{3}{4}$ to one hour
Tuesday	A 1 to 1 $\frac{1}{2}$ hours
Wednesday	L 5,000 m
Thursday	A one to 1 $\frac{1}{2}$ hours
Friday	F 100 m x 8-10
Saturday	L 5,000 m
Sunday	A 1 $\frac{1}{2}$ hours or more

For four weeks:

Monday	DE $\frac{3}{4}$ hour
Tuesday	A one to 1 $\frac{1}{2}$ hours
Wednesday	L 5,000 m
Thursday	DE $\frac{3}{4}$ hour
Friday	F 100 m x 8-10
Saturday	L 5,000 m
Sunday	A 1 $\frac{1}{2}$ hours or more

For four weeks:

Monday	J x 6-8
Tuesday	B $\frac{3}{4}$ to 1 hour
Wednesday	L 3,000 m
Thursday	K 200 m x 8-10
Friday	N 300 m x 4
Saturday	Development races
Sunday	A 1 $\frac{1}{2}$ hours or more

For one week:

Monday	H x 16
Tuesday	B $\frac{3}{4}$ to one hour
Wednesday	L 3,000 m
Thursday	K 300 m fast x 3
Friday	W $\frac{1}{2}$ hour
Saturday	Race 5,000 m
Sunday	W 1 to 1 $\frac{1}{2}$ hours

For one week:

Monday	H x 16
Tuesday	B $\frac{3}{4}$ hour
Wednesday	L 2,000 m
Thursday	B $\frac{1}{2}$ hour
Friday	O 200 m x 3
Saturday	Race 3,000 m
Sunday	W one hour

For one week:

Monday	H x 12
Tuesday	B $\frac{1}{2}$ to $\frac{3}{4}$ hour
Wednesday	L 1,500 m
Thursday	W $\frac{3}{4}$ hour
Friday	W $\frac{1}{2}$ hour
Saturday	First important race
Sunday	W one to 1 $\frac{1}{2}$ hours

Continuation of racing:

Monday	H x 12-16
Tuesday	B $\frac{3}{4}$ hour
Wednesday	L 3,000 m
Thursday	B $\frac{1}{2}$ hour
Friday	W $\frac{1}{2}$ hour
Saturday	Race
Sunday	W one to 1 $\frac{1}{2}$ hour

Cross-country – men, 18 and 19

For as long as possible:

Monday	B one hour
Tuesday	A one to 1 $\frac{1}{2}$ hours
Wednesday	L 5,000 m
Thursday	A one to 1 $\frac{1}{2}$ hours
Friday	F 100 m x 10
Saturday	L 10,000 m
Sunday	A 1 $\frac{1}{2}$ hours or more

For four weeks:

Monday	DE $\frac{3}{4}$ to one hour
Tuesday	A one to 1 $\frac{1}{2}$ hours
Wednesday	L 5,000 m
Thursday	DE $\frac{3}{4}$ to one hour
Friday	F 100 m x 10
Saturday	L 5,000 m
Sunday	A 1 $\frac{1}{2}$ hours or more

For four weeks:

Monday	J x 8-12
Tuesday	B one hour
Wednesday	L 5,000 m
Thursday	K 200 m x 10-12
Friday	N 200 m x 4
Saturday	Development races
Sunday	A 1 $\frac{1}{2}$ hours or more

For one week:

Monday	H x 16-20
Tuesday	B one hour
Wednesday	L 3,000 m
Thursday	B $\frac{3}{4}$ hour
Friday	W $\frac{1}{2}$ hour
Saturday	Race 5,000 m
Sunday	W 1 $\frac{1}{2}$ hours

For one week:

Monday	H x 16
Tuesday	B ¾ hour
Wednesday	L 2,000 m
Thursday	B ½ hour
Friday	O 200 m x 3
Saturday	Race 3,000 m
Sunday	W one hour

For one week:

Monday	H x 16
Tuesday	B ¾ hour
Wednesday	L 1,500 m
Thursday	W ¾ hour
Friday	W ½ hour
Saturday	First important race
Sunday	W 1 ½ hours

Continuation of racing:

Monday	H x 16
Tuesday	B ¾ hour
Wednesday	L 3,000 m
Thursday	B ½ hour
Friday	W ½ hour
Saturday	Race
Sunday	W 1 ½ hours

Cross-country – men

For as long as possible:

Monday	B one hour
Tuesday	A 1 ½ hours
Wednesday	L 5,000 m
Thursday	A 1 ½ hours
Friday	F 100 m x 10
Saturday	L 10,000 m
Sunday	A two hours or more

For four weeks:

Monday	DE 1 hour
Tuesday	A 1 $\frac{1}{2}$ hour
Wednesday	L 5,000 m
Thursday	DE one hour
Friday	G 100 m x 10
Saturday	L 10,000 m
Sunday	A two hours or more

For four weeks:

Monday	J x 10-12
Tuesday	B one hour
Wednesday	L 5,000 m
Thursday	K 200 m x 10-15
Friday	N 300 m x 4
Saturday	Development races
Sunday	A two hours

For one week:

Monday	H x 20
Tuesday	B one hour
Wednesday	L 3,000 m
Thursday	B $\frac{3}{4}$ hour
Friday	W $\frac{1}{2}$ hour
Saturday	Race 10,000 m
Sunday	W 1 $\frac{1}{2}$ hours

For one week:

Monday	H x 20
Tuesday	B $\frac{3}{4}$ hour
Wednesday	L 2,000 m
Thursday	B $\frac{1}{2}$ hour
Friday	O 200 m x 3
Saturday	Race 3,000 m
Sunday	W one hour

For one week:

Monday	H x 16
Tuesday	B $3/4$ hour
Wednesday	L 1,500 m
Thursday	W $3/4$ hour
Friday	W $1/2$ hour
Saturday	First important race
Sunday	W 1 $1/2$ hours

Continuation of racing:

Monday	H x 16
Tuesday	B $3/4$ hour
Wednesday	L 3,000 m
Thursday	B $1/2$ hour
Friday	W $1/2$ hour
Saturday	Race
Sunday	W 1 $1/2$ hours or more

Cross-country – girls, under 12

For as long as possible:

Monday	A $1/4$ to $1/2$ hour
Tuesday	B $1/4$ to $1/2$ hour
Wednesday	L 2,000 m
Thursday	A $1/4$ to $1/2$ hour
Friday	W $1/4$ hour or rest
Saturday	L 2,000 m
Sunday	A 20 minutes or more

For four weeks:

Monday	B $1/4$ to $1/2$ hour
Tuesday	A $1/4$ to $1/2$ hour
Wednesday	L 2,000 m
Thursday	N 150 m x 4
Friday	W $1/4$ hour or rest
Saturday	L 2,000 m
Sunday	A 20 minutes or more

For four weeks:

Monday	H x 6-8
Tuesday	B $\frac{1}{4}$ to $\frac{1}{2}$ hour
Wednesday	L 1,500 m
Thursday	B $\frac{1}{4}$ to $\frac{1}{2}$ hour
Friday	W $\frac{1}{4}$ hour or rest
Saturday	Development races
Sunday	W $\frac{1}{2}$ hour

For one week:

Monday	H x 6-8
Tuesday	B $\frac{1}{4}$ to $\frac{1}{2}$ hour
Wednesday	L 800 m
Thursday	N 150 m x 3
Friday	W $\frac{1}{4}$ hour or rest
Saturday	Race 2,000 m
Sunday	W $\frac{1}{2}$ hour

For one week:

Monday	H x 6-8
Tuesday	B $\frac{1}{4}$ to $\frac{1}{2}$ hour
Wednesday	L 600 m
Thursday	W $\frac{1}{4}$ hour
Friday	W $\frac{1}{4}$ hour or rest
Saturday	Race 1,000 m
Sunday	W $\frac{1}{2}$ hour

For one week:

Monday	H x 6
Tuesday	W $\frac{1}{4}$ hour
Wednesday	L 600 m
Thursday	W $\frac{1}{4}$ hour
Friday	Rest
Saturday	First important race
Sunday	W $\frac{1}{2}$ hour

Continuation of racing:

Monday	H x 6
Tuesday	B $\frac{1}{4}$ to $\frac{1}{2}$ hour
Wednesday	L 800 m
Thursday	B $\frac{1}{4}$ to $\frac{1}{2}$ hour
Friday	W $\frac{1}{4}$ hour or rest
Saturday	Race
Sunday	W $\frac{1}{2}$ hour

Cross-country – girls, 12 and 13 years

For as long as possible:

Monday	A $\frac{1}{2}$ to $\frac{3}{4}$ hour
Tuesday	B $\frac{1}{4}$ to $\frac{1}{2}$ hour
Wednesday	L 2,500 m
Thursday	A $\frac{1}{2}$ to $\frac{3}{4}$ hour
Friday	F 80 m x 4-6
Saturday	L 3,000 m
Sunday	A $\frac{1}{2}$ hour or more

For four weeks:

Monday	DE $\frac{1}{4}$ hour
Tuesday	A $\frac{1}{2}$ to $\frac{3}{4}$ hour
Wednesday	L 2,500 m
Thursday	K 200 m x 4-6
Friday	F 80 m x 4-6
Saturday	L 3,000 m
Sunday	A 1/2 hour or more

For four weeks:

Monday	J x 4-6
Tuesday	B $\frac{1}{4}$ to $\frac{1}{2}$ hour
Wednesday	L 2,000 m
Thursday	B $\frac{1}{4}$ to $\frac{1}{2}$ hour
Friday	W $\frac{1}{4}$ hour or rest
Saturday	Development races
Sunday	A $\frac{1}{2}$ hour or more

For one week:

Monday	H x 8-10
Tuesday	B $\frac{1}{4}$ to $\frac{1}{2}$ hour
Wednesday	L 800 m
Thursday	N 150 m x 3
Friday	W $\frac{1}{4}$ hour or rest
Saturday	Race 2,000 m
Sunday	W $\frac{1}{2}$ hour or more

For one week:

Monday	H x 6-8
Tuesday	B $\frac{1}{4}$ to $\frac{1}{2}$ hour
Wednesday	L 600 m
Thursday	B $\frac{1}{4}$ to $\frac{1}{2}$ hour
Friday	W $\frac{1}{4}$ hour or rest
Saturday	Race 1,000 m
Sunday	W $\frac{1}{2}$ hour

For one week:

Monday	H x 6
Tuesday	W $\frac{1}{2}$ hour
Wednesday	L 600 m
Thursday	W $\frac{1}{4}$ hour
Friday	Rest
Saturday	First important race
Sunday	W $\frac{1}{2}$ hour or more

Continuation of racing:

Monday	H x 6-8
Tuesday	B $\frac{1}{4}$ to $\frac{1}{2}$ hour
Wednesday	L 600 m
Thursday	B $\frac{1}{4}$ to $\frac{1}{2}$ hour
Friday	W $\frac{1}{4}$ hour or rest
Saturday	Race
Sunday	W $\frac{1}{2}$ hour or more

Cross-country – girls, 14 to 15 years

For as long as possible:

Monday	B $\frac{1}{2}$ hour
Tuesday	A $\frac{3}{4}$ to one hour
Wednesday	L 3,000 m
Thursday	A $\frac{3}{4}$ to one hour
Friday	F 80 m x 4-6
Saturday	L 3,000 m
Sunday	A $\frac{3}{4}$ hour or more

For four weeks:

Monday	DE $\frac{1}{2}$ hour
Tuesday	A $\frac{3}{4}$ to one hour
Wednesday	L 3,000 m
Thursday	K 200 m x 6-8
Friday	F 80 m x 6-8
Saturday	L 3,000 m or club run
Sunday	A $\frac{3}{4}$ hour or more

For four weeks:

Monday	J x 6-8
Tuesday	B $\frac{1}{2}$ to $\frac{3}{4}$ hour
Wednesday	L 2,000 m
Thursday	B $\frac{1}{2}$ hour
Friday	N 200 m x 4
Saturday	Development races
Sunday	A $\frac{3}{4}$ hour or more

For one week:

Monday	H x 8-10
Tuesday	B $\frac{1}{2}$ hour
Wednesday	L 1,000 m
Thursday	B $\frac{1}{2}$ hour
Friday	W $\frac{1}{2}$ hour
Saturday	Race 2,500 m
Sunday	W $\frac{3}{4}$ to one hour

For one week:

Monday	H x 6-8
Tuesday	B $\frac{1}{2}$ hour
Wednesday	L 800 m
Thursday	B $\frac{1}{2}$ hour
Friday	N 200 m x 3
Saturday	Race 1,000 m
Sunday	W $\frac{3}{4}$ hour

For one week:

Monday	H x 6
Tuesday	B $\frac{1}{2}$ hour
Wednesday	L 600 m
Thursday	W $\frac{1}{2}$ hour
Friday	W $\frac{1}{4}$ hour or rest
Saturday	First important race
Sunday	W one hour

Continuation of racing:

Monday	H x 6-8
Tuesday	B $\frac{1}{2}$ to $\frac{3}{4}$ hour
Wednesday	L 800 m or 1,000 m
Thursday	B $\frac{1}{2}$ hour
Friday	W $\frac{1}{2}$ hour
Saturday	Race
Sunday	W one hour

Cross-country – women, 16 to 17 years

For as long as possible:

Monday	B $\frac{3}{4}$ hour
Tuesday	A one hour or more
Wednesday	L 4,000 m
Thursday	A one hour or more
Friday	F 80 m x 6-8
Saturday	L 5,000 m
Sunday	A one hour or more

For four weeks:

Monday	DE $\frac{1}{2}$ to $\frac{3}{4}$ hour
Tuesday	A one hour or more
Wednesday	L 3,000 m
Thursday	K 200 m x 8-10
Friday	F 80 m x 8-10
Saturday	L 4,000 m
Sunday	A one hour or more

For four weeks:

Monday	J x 6-8
Tuesday	B $\frac{3}{4}$ hour
Wednesday	L 3,000 m
Thursday	B $\frac{1}{2}$ hour
Friday	N 200 m x 4-6
Saturday	Development races
Sunday	A one hour or more

For one week:

Monday	H x 12-16
Tuesday	B $\frac{3}{4}$ hour
Wednesday	L 1,500 m
Thursday	B $\frac{1}{2}$ hour
Friday	W $\frac{1}{2}$ hour
Saturday	Race 3,000 m
Sunday	W one hour

For one week:

Monday	H x 12-16
Tuesday	B $\frac{3}{4}$ hour
Wednesday	L 1,000 m
Thursday	B $\frac{1}{2}$ hour
Friday	N 200 m x 3
Saturday	Race 2,000 m
Sunday	W one hour

For one week:

Monday	H x 12
Tuesday	B $\frac{1}{2}$ hour
Wednesday	L 600 m
Thursday	W $\frac{1}{2}$ hour
Friday	W $\frac{1}{2}$ hour or rest
Saturday	First important race
Sunday	W one hour

Continuation of racing:

Monday	H x 6-8
Tuesday	B $\frac{1}{2}$ to $\frac{3}{4}$ hour
Wednesday	L 1,000 m
Thursday	B $\frac{1}{2}$ hour
Friday	W $\frac{1}{2}$ hour
Saturday	Race
Sunday	W one hour or more

Cross-country – senior women

For as long as possible:

Monday	B $\frac{3}{4}$ to one hour
Tuesday	A one to 1 $\frac{1}{2}$ hour
Wednesday	L 5,000 m
Thursday	A one to 1 $\frac{1}{2}$ hour
Friday	F 100 m x 8-10
Saturday	L 5,000 m
Sunday	A 1 $\frac{1}{2}$ hours or more

For four weeks:

Monday	DE $\frac{3}{4}$ to one hour
Tuesday	A one to 1 $\frac{1}{2}$ hours
Wednesday	L 3,000 m
Thursday	DE $\frac{3}{4}$ to one hour
Friday	F 100 m x 8-10
Saturday	L 5,000 m
Sunday	A $\frac{1}{2}$ hours or more

For four weeks:

Monday	J 100 m x 10-12
Tuesday	B $\frac{3}{4}$ to one hour
Wednesday	L 3,000 m
Thursday	K 300 m fast
Friday	N 300 m x 4
Saturday	Development races
Sunday	A 1 $\frac{1}{2}$ hours or more

For one week:

Monday	H x 16-20
Tuesday	B $\frac{3}{4}$ to one hour
Wednesday	L 2,000 m
Thursday	B $\frac{3}{4}$ hour
Friday	W $\frac{1}{2}$ hour
Saturday	Race 5,000 m
Sunday	W one hour

For one week:

Monday	H x 16
Tuesday	B $\frac{3}{4}$ hour
Wednesday	L 2,000 m
Thursday	B $\frac{1}{2}$ hour
Friday	O 200 m x 3
Saturday	Race 2,000 m
Sunday	W one hour

For one week:

Monday	H x 16
Tuesday	B $\frac{1}{2}$ hour
Wednesday	L 1,000 m
Thursday	W $\frac{3}{4}$ hour
Friday	W $\frac{1}{2}$ hour
Saturday	First important race
Sunday	W 1 $\frac{1}{2}$ hours

Continuation of racing:

Monday	H x 16
Tuesday	B $\frac{3}{4}$ hour
Wednesday	L 3,000 m
Thursday	B $\frac{1}{2}$ hour
Friday	W $\frac{1}{2}$ hour
Saturday	Race
Sunday	W one hour or more

Marathon

The point of marathon training is to develop fine general cardiac efficiency, which basically means the improved intake, transportation and use of oxygen. With continued running, the intake and transportstion improve quickly but the improved use of oxygenby the muscles takes longer. This necessary development of muscular endurance can only be achieved through the continuous exercise of muscle groups for long periods.

Muscle group exercise, particularly for two hours or more, not only affects underdeveloped capillary beds but develops new beds, giving an important increase in muscular endurance. So, successful marathon running or racing means long runs often, the more the better. The end result is more efficient blood sugar usage and waste product elimination.

The nucleus of the training programme is three long runs a week, interchanged with other runs which, while they can be shorter, are usually over hilly terrain. Because marathons are run most of the way at fast but aerobic speeds, there is normally little need to do a lot of anaerobic training – the 5,000 and 10,000 metres time trials are enough to develop the anaerobic capacity.

Fartlek, the mixture of all sorts of running over country is of value, provided you vary your mixture according to how you feel on the day.

When you begin marathon training, train on a time basis rather than set out to cover a specific mileage. This lets you feel your way and removes the compulsion to overdo it; it also allows you to run out anywhere, without a predetermined course, which can make the long time on your feet a whole lot more interesting. If you follow a regular route, you are inclined to stage time yourself and even become competitive with yourself. The temptation to clip some time off your last run over the course or perhaps go for a personal best because you are feeling good on the day is enough to destroy the basic objective of the training run. It can edge you into anaerobic running.

The same caution applies if you are running in the company of others. You must always run to your fitness level, not anyone else's. In conditioning training, you can never run too slowly to improve the oxygen uptake; but you can run too fast.

Getting used to running in the heat is important; if you are not prepared for it, you can suffer ill-effects. Hot weather training develops the skin arterioles more to allow more blood to be pumped to the skin surface for cooling. Sauna baths can help in this development, but do not stay in them too long.

Always train and race well within your capabilities. Start at a steady effort and do not be trapped into going too fast at the beginning.

A modified marathon schedule for women is included in a following chapter, "Women in Training".

Take careful note of this 18-point marathon race check list, particularly if you are new to the competitive distance:

1. Keep to your normal balanced meals the days before the race. Protein, carbohydrate and fat are all necessary for a balanced metabolism in a marathon race.

2. Eat up to eight oz of honey or sugars supplementary to your normal meals during the two days before the race.

3. Finish eating about three hours before the start, if possible, or eat sparingly.

4. Eat a light breakfast, preferably of cereals, honey and toast with tea or coffee.

5. Have good fitting shoes and clothes that will not chafe, and are suitable for the conditions of the day.

6. Use lubricant (olive oil, lanolin) under arms and crotch and on nipples.

7. When you put on your running shoes, force your heels hard into the backs of the shoes before lacing firmly, but not too tight. This will stop the foot movement that leads to blistering and the loss of your toenails.

8. Do not run much before the start. Save your energy.

9. Stretch and loosen a little.

10. Start well within your capabilities and warm up to the run as you go. Hold yourself in check, it will pay off later.

11. Do not exaggerate your knee lift. From the start, try to relax and not lift the knees higher than necessary. You must save the muscles that lift the legs.

12. Ignore the other runners. Run at efforts that suit you.

13. Prepare electrolyte drinks for a hot day. Sustalyte or Thirst-Aid are two, but make the mixture weaker than directed and add some honey.

14. Do not take salt tablets, though potassium to protect against heat is recommended.

15. Drink water or electrolyte drinks throughout the race on a hot day. A glass just before the start can help. If you do not have a proper drinking vessel, stop to drink to avoid gulping air.

16. Keep your body wet. Sponging is the best insurance against dehydration and high body temperatures.
    Trim a sponge to fit into your hand and tape it there to carry water between water stations.

17. Do not surge during the race and waste energy.

18. Do not use anti-perspirants. You need to sweat.

Note

A - Long aerobic running

B - Easy fartlek running

C - Strong fartlek running

D - Hill springing

E - Steep hills or step running

F - Leg speed

G - Sprint training

H - 45-metre windsprints every 100 metres

J - 100-metre windsprints every 200 metres

K - Repetitions

L - Time trials

M - Pace judgement running

N - Relaxed striding

O - Fast relaxed running

P - High knee-lift exercise

Q - Long striding exercising

R - Running tall exercising

S - Calisthenics

T - Skipping

U - Cycling

V - Swimming

W - Jogging

X - Sprints starts

Y - Hurdles practice

Z - Water jump practice

Marathon – beginners

For as long as possible:

Monday	A $\frac{1}{2}$ to $\frac{3}{4}$ hour
Tuesday	A one hour
Wednesday	A $\frac{1}{2}$ to $\frac{3}{4}$ hour
Thursday	A one hour
Friday	A $\frac{1}{2}$ to $\frac{3}{4}$ hour
Saturday	A one to two hours
Sunday	A $\frac{3}{4}$ to one hour

For six weeks:

Monday	A $\frac{3}{4}$ to one hour
Tuesday	A one to 1 $\frac{1}{2}$ hours
Wednesday	B $\frac{1}{2}$ to $\frac{3}{4}$ hour
Thursday	A one to 1 $\frac{1}{2}$ hours
Friday	B $\frac{1}{2}$ hour
Saturday	A 1 $\frac{1}{2}$ hour to two hours
Sunday	A $\frac{3}{4}$ to one hour

For six weeks:

Monday	L 5,000 m
Tuesday	A one to 1 $\frac{1}{2}$ hours
Wednesday	L 10,000m
Thursday	A one to 1 $\frac{1}{2}$ hours
Friday	B $\frac{1}{2}$ to $\frac{3}{4}$ hour
Saturday	A 1 $\frac{1}{2}$ to 2 $\frac{1}{2}$ hours
Sunday	W one hour

For four weeks:

Monday	O 200 m x 8
Tuesday	A one to 1 $\frac{1}{2}$ hours
Wednesday	L 5,000 m
Thursday	B $\frac{1}{2}$ to one hour
Friday	N 200 m x 6
Saturday	A 1 $\frac{1}{2}$ to 2 $\frac{1}{2}$ hours
Sunday	W one hour

For one week:

Monday	B $\frac{1}{2}$ to $\frac{3}{4}$ hour
Tuesday	A one hour
Wednesday	L 3,000 m
Thursday	B $\frac{1}{2}$ to $\frac{3}{4}$ hour
Friday	W $\frac{1}{2}$ hour
Saturday	A one hour
Sunday	B $\frac{1}{2}$ hour

For one week:

Monday	W $\frac{3}{4}$ hour
Tuesday	L 2,000 m
Wednesday	W $\frac{3}{4}$ hour
Thursday	W $\frac{3}{4}$ hour
Friday	W $\frac{1}{2}$ hour or rest
Saturday	Your marathon race
Sunday	W $\frac{3}{4}$ to one hour

Continuation: Jog easily for seven to ten days, then:

Monday	B $\frac{3}{4}$ to one hour
Tuesday	A one to 1 $\frac{1}{2}$ hours
Wednesday	L 3,000 m
Thursday	A one to 1 $\frac{1}{2}$ hours
Friday	W one hour
Saturday	5,000 m
Sunday	1 $\frac{1}{2}$ hours or more

Marathon – experienced runners

For as long as possible:

Monday	A one hour
Tuesday	A 1 $\frac{1}{2}$ hours
Wednesday	B one hour on hills
Thursday	A 1 $\frac{1}{2}$ hours
Friday	W one hour
Saturday	A two hours or more
Sunday	A 1 $\frac{1}{2}$ hours

For four weeks:

Monday	DE 1 hour
Tuesday	A 1 $\frac{1}{2}$ hours
Wednesday	L 5,000 m
Thursday	D and E one hour
Friday	F 100 m x 10
Saturday	B one hour
Sunday	A two hours or more

For four weeks:

Monday	K 200 m x 15-20
Tuesday	A 1 $\frac{1}{2}$ hours
Wednesday	L 5,000 m
Thursday	B 1 hour
Friday	F 100 m x 10
Saturday	L 10,000 m
Sunday	A two hours or more

For two weeks:

Monday	J x 10-12
Tuesday	A 1 $\frac{1}{2}$ hours
Wednesday	L 5,000 m
Thursday	A 1 $\frac{1}{2}$ hours
Friday	B $\frac{1}{2}$ hour
Saturday	L 25 km
Sunday	W 1 $\frac{1}{2}$ hours

For one week:

Monday	J x 10-12
Tuesday	A 1 $\frac{1}{2}$ hours
Wednesday	L 3,000 m
Thursday	B one hour
Friday	W $\frac{1}{2}$ hour
Saturday	L 20 km
Sunday	W 1 $\frac{1}{2}$ hours

For one week:

Monday	H x 20
Tuesday	B $\frac{3}{4}$ hour
Wednesday	W one hour
Thursday	W one hour
Friday	W $\frac{1}{2}$ hour
Saturday	L full marathon
Sunday	W one hour

For one week:

Monday	W one hour
Tuesday	W one hour
Wednesday	L 5,000 m
Thursday	W 1 $\frac{1}{2}$ hours
Friday	W one hour
Saturday	L 5,000 m
Sunday	A two hours

For one week:

Monday	J x 10
Tuesday	A 1 $\frac{1}{2}$ hours
Wednesday	L 3,000 m
Thursday	B one hour
Friday	W $\frac{1}{2}$ hour
Saturday	L 10,000 m
Sunday	W 1 $\frac{1}{2}$ hours

For one week:

Monday	B x 20
Tuesday	B one hour
Wednesday	L 3,000 m
Thursday	W one hour
Friday	W $\frac{1}{2}$ hour
Saturday	L 5,000 m
Sunday	W 1 $\frac{1}{2}$ hours

For one week:

Monday	B $\frac{3}{4}$ hour
Tuesday	L 2,000 m
Wednesday	W one hour
Thursday	W $\frac{1}{2}$ hour
Friday	W $\frac{1}{2}$ hour or rest
Saturday	Marathon race
Sunday	W one hour

Continuation (recovery):

Monday	W one hour
Tuesday	W 1 $\frac{1}{2}$ hours
Wednesday	W one hour
Thursday	B one hour
Friday	W $\frac{1}{2}$ hour
Saturday	W one hour
Sunday	W 1 $\frac{1}{2}$ hours

Continuation (race track):

Monday	J x 10
Tuesday	A 1 $\frac{1}{2}$ hours
Wednesday	L 3,000 m
Thursday	B one hour
Friday	W $\frac{1}{2}$ hour
Saturday	Race 5 km or 10 km
Sunday	A 1 $\frac{1}{2}$ hours or more

13   Running for Boys and Girls

At what age should youngsters begin running and training? From my experience and from research and experience in many countries, seven seems to be the age from which boys and girls can absorb large amounts of long distance running without any undesirable effects.

Youngsters under 15 can handle a great deal of aerobic training because their capacity to use oxygen in relation to their body weight is greater than an adult's. However, they usually have highly sensitive nervous systems and cannot stand much anaerobic training. It is not unusual for boys and girls of ten to twelve to run weekly mileages of up to 120 and even 160 kilometres and to continue to improve athletically.

Competitive racing cannot harm youngsters of any age, provided the races are limited in distance – sprints up to 200 metres and middle or distance races of 800 metres and upwards. It is usually the prolonged sprints of 300 to 400 metres that cause problems because the oxygen debts incurred through sustained speed running are often more than they can handle. These are the distances which cause youngsters to be sick, to black out or to suffer distress afterwards. Most youngsters can run 200 metres quite fast but, by then, they are into a big oxygen debt. In a 400 metres race, this would mean they would be exhausted at the entrance to the finishing straight, the danger point at which they could commit themselves or be coerced into forcing themselves and overdoing it.

The 800 metres is a different story. Youngsters recognise it is not a sprint and will settle at a pace they can manage without distressing themselves abnormally.

New Zealand youngsters run cross-country from an early age. Boys are into the 3,000 to 5,000 metres runs from about eight onwards, which may seem a tremendous demand but we have proved that as long as their hearts are sound they will come to no harm at all. It is sustained speed, not sustained running, that does the damage; a difference of emphasis which, when overlooked, has wrecked many potential champions over the years in more countries than New Zealand.

I always remember the words of Gundar HAEGG'S coach, HOLMAR: *"If you can get a boy in his teens and encourage him to train and not race until he is matured, then you have laid the foundations of an Olympic champion."*

I believe that sums the whole thing up. Encourage the young athlete, do not force him or her. Let them play at and with athletics. If you can keep them in that frame of mind and dampen down their early competitiveness and, with it, any discouragement over defeat, their capacity for exercise and the benefits they draw from it will astound you.

I have watched thousands of boys and girls running in cross-country packs, jumping creeks and fences, ploughing through mud, in fresh air, sunshine and rain, enjoying a sport that recognises none of the confines of the measured field. I have yet to see one of them fall in an exhausted heap; but all of them are conditioning themselves for more serious running later.

One of the great advantages of cross-country running is that parents cannot follow alongside and urge their children to faster speeds and greater effort than they are physically or mentally prepared for. The parental influence on sport can be a wonderful contribution but it can also be a real danger, even a destroyer. Too many parents are more interested in seeing their children beat every other kid than in encouraging them simply to enjoy themselves. They force the child to show superiority, but it is at that child's expense, not at the expense of those he or she beats.

Schedule training can be applied to the young runner most successfully. Many Auckland youngsters include the 35-kilometre Waitakere Ranges circuit, over which SNELL, HALBERG, MAGEE and my other runners trained, in their week's running quite regularly: at the pace of their own choosing and without discomfort. Is is a steep hill training circuit which is regarded as most formidable even by mature runners but they enjoy it because the only pressure they apply is that chosen by themselves and always within their capacity.

Girls, from puberty through to about 15, and boys, from puberty to about 17 or 18, have a lot of natural endurance which enables them to perform well, often without a lot of training. After that, natural endurance ceases to develop and, unless the young runner is prepared to put in the aerobic mileage, he or she will not continue to improve. This is why we often see boys and girls performing exceptionally well and beating many runners who train harder until, at 16 for girls and 18-19 for boys, the hard workers begin to go past them and eventually stay there.

It has become apparent that girls and women can train to the same volume and intensity as boys and men though, because of their muscular endurance, they cannot achieve the same ultimate performance levels. It has also been convincingly proved now that training with the same intensity and volume as men does not have the slightest effect on their femininity. Hormones do not change; women who have trained all their lives are only improved in appearance.

14   Women in Training

It has taken administrators a long time to promote and even allow women's middle and distance events; even now there remains some resistance to them running farther than 1,500 metres but the Olympics have finally featured a 3,000 metres race for women and they have burst into the serious marathon running area with a vengeance in recent years. There is no physiological reason why women should not run the marathon and it has been convincingly demonstrated recently that they can run it aggressively and well.

But, only in 1973, I watched a schoolgirls' 800 metres race in Auckland which was open to all ages from 13 to 19. No other middle distance race was provided for the 13-years-old girls so, if they were not fast enough for the shorter events and they wanted to compete, they were forced to run against much more mature girls. One 13-year-old collapsed after the first lap because the pace set by the older girls was much too fast for her.

I remarked to a teacher who was on the committee which planned the programme that she was responsible for the girl's collapse because of the unrealistic approach the committee had made to the programme; I was pleased to note that, in the following years, middle-distance races were included for the various age-groups.

But girls of all secondary school ages need longer races, such as the 3,000 metres. How else are the younger and slower ones going to be encouraged to train for and participate in a sport that can only do them a lot of good? There could well be a champion among those who are not catered for because they are not natural sprinters.

Today, women all around the world are producing fine middle and distance performances, particularly from Russia, Germany and Bulgaria, whose women have approached their training as men do and are running up to 200 kilometres a week. Comparatively, women runners in many other countries are not doing a sufficient volume of training. Nor, I suggest, do they watch their weight as carefully.

In *Run the Lydiard Way*, published in 1978, we noted that women were already running the marathon in times under 2:40; I also predicted they would soon get under 2:30. It took the first of them, in fact, only two years to do that. There is nothing surprising about it because, once women began accepting that, physically, they were capable of racing, not merely running, a marathon, the improvement had to be rapid.

Fortunately, there is not so much talk these days about women athletes becoming some sort of Amazons through running long distances. It is both mythical and physiologically incorrect. Women do not become masculine and develop bulky muscles through running. Why should they? Men do not. Many of the world's best women athletes are extremely feminine and attractive even though they train like men and perform at the highest levels.

The physique is the basic form and structure of the body, compounded of bone, muscle and fat. The female can never develop muscles as strong as the male, so resistance and strength training will never produce male-like firmness of muscles nor increase muscle size to the same extent. Muscle fibres cannot be increased. Women, therefore, have little to fear.

The inherent anatomical attributes of the female enable her to excel in sports, rather than any tendency to masculinity or predominance of male characteristics. She excels because she has been endowed with a body which enables her to perform with greater skill, if with less sheer strength.

In the marathon, for instance, it is becoming recognised that the woman is at some advantage because she has a greater proportion of muscle fat than the male, which enables her to draw out her reserves far more efficiently and may well eliminate that dreaded 'wall' that so many runners hit at 20 miles (32 kilometres) or so, when body reserves run out and the debt begins to build. Women certainly seem to finish in an apparently fresher state than men and, in times, they are getting rapidly nearer the front in increasing numbers.

Many fallacies surround the influence of exercise and sports participation on menstruation. It has been generally accepted that women should avoid vigorous activity before, during and after their period; but it is a general conclusion not based on fact. Menstruation is a biological phenomenon which places a particular burden on the blood production system and it was, therefore, assumed that any additional physical stress on the organism during this period would overload to some extent the physiological function and disturb the cycle in some harmful way.

Changes do take place but it has been established that they vary from individual to individual, and from beneficial to harmful. In other words, it is entirely an individual matter; activity which upsets one woman need not necessarily upset another. Research suggests that vigorous activity, even to the point of voluntary fatigue, will benefit as many as it will harm in terms of length and volume of menstrual flow.

It is now accepted that the direction of the changes seems to be related to the mental and physical characteristics and status of the female, so that restriction of physical activity during menstruation should not be a generally applied principle but one applied with discretion and with regard to each individual case.

Anyone who measures up to the following general requirements should not need to restrict activity during menstruation: enjoys good health; is physically fit and in condition to do the specific activity; does not perform exercises that require excessive abdominal contraction and compression or cause excessive shock to or bouncing of the organism; does not perform activities that require explosive action, such as the shot put and discus; avoids extreme heat or cold; is not compelled or coerced into participation against her will.

Equally, modern biological and medical evidence now indicates that the female benefits during childbirth and in the post-parturition period from competitive sports and exercise.

The female, in addition to a lighter and weaker build with less muscle bulk which makes her generally about one-third less strong than the male in either individual muscle or total strength capacity, also has a cardio-pulmonary reserve capacity about two-thirds that of the male. She is therefore unable to obtain the same maximal oxygen intake, ventilation volume and cardiac output as the male during physical performance.

Her loosely constructed abdominal organs, the inclined pelvis, producing a great abdominal area, and the pelvic floor constitute weaknesses in her physique but, in spite of this, she has the qualities and all the physiological capacities to enable her to perform the same types of movements and engage in the same physical activities as the male. She is limited only by intensity and strength. At her own level, she can match the male in activities requiring speed, strength, endurance and skill.

When I first trained young men in their teens, I was cautious about the amount of training I could give them. I knew what a man could stand and still improve but I did not know what a youth could take without impairing his performance. After years of experimentation, I concluded that boys could run up to 160 kilometres a week, as long as the speed was controlled to an economic level, and that they could stand as much supplementary jogging as well. The same is now happening in the training of women; at their own level, they can train as long as men.

Women beginning training should jog daily on grass – parks and golf courses are ideal – to allow their muscles to tone up comfortably while the respiratory and circulatory systems are being conditioned. Fifteen minutes a day is enough to begin with but, once the initial soreness has disappeared from the muscles, the running should be increased to provide a longer run every second or third day. All daily times can then be extended as long as the balance is maintained between long runs and alternating short runs to allow for recovery and improvement.

This is easier than it may seem because the body's reaction to this training is a spectacularly rapid improvement in stamina and general condition. Cross-country training and races should be brought into the system before the runner progresses to a conditioning schedule, resistance training and track work, which place more demands on the body's resources and depend for success on the quick recovery which only adequate stamina and strong condition give.

Schedules for women are included in this book but their schedule for marathon-type training should be modified from the men's schedule to something like this:

Monday:	One hour's steady running
Tuesday:	Half-hour fartlek
Wednesday:	One and a half hours' steady running
Thursday:	One hour's steady running
Friday:	Half-hour fartlek
Saturday:	One and a half hours' steady running
Sunday:	One hour's steady running.

The fartlek or speed play should include more stride-outs than sprints. During the half hour, mostly run at an even pace, stride out periodically for any distance up to 200 metres, occasionally increase speed on uphill slopes and stride out easily on downhill slopes, provided they are not too steep.

15   Ball Games and Team Training

The great majority of team players present themselves to their coaches at the beginning of a season in the blind belief that dear old 'coach' is going to get them fit, teach them and polish the basics of their game and play them competitively, all at one and at the same time – successfully. This is a bit like trying to make a silk purse from a pig's ear or trying to win a Grand Prix with a model T.

What, in fact, do we get? On the eve of the season, a crash course in running – and if there are hills around the training ground the crashes come fast and heavy – and in sprinting and in basic game techniques. All are crowded into viciously vigorous sessions which tend to produce, in the main, exactly the wrong kind of physical condition (measured in terms of aching muscles) which can lead to early serious injury, to mid-season staleness and, at best, to a mediocre all-season effort in which true fitness is always a wish away.

Fortunately, the trend is steadily away from this masochistic approach to the enjoyment of sport. You do not now see quite as many oddly garbed ball players trudging their summer stomachs along the streets and around the park perimeters, gasping in the gathering dusk, overdressed in a desperate effort to get the surplus weight off. You do not see quite as many of those half-hearted sprint sessions on the training paddock by groups of athletes who submit themselves to pressure they cannot sustain in a desperate effort to get ready for the first game of the season.

In the past, though, it was not too bad. Any other team you were likely to meet early in the season could be expected to be in the same semi-prepared state, so it all evened out. You could safely gamble that when you kicked the ball out of the field of play or delayed a movement to give yourself and your team-mates a breather, the other side would be just as relieved and you could all stand about, hands on knees, gulping for oxygen in a great spirit of companionable suffering. The secret was, if you had the strength left, to kick the ball as far as possible into the stands or the next paddock and hope that whoever went to fetch it took his time.

In the sphere of amateur sport played, theoretically, for fun, this may not seem a situation of much concern. But when the same circumstances apply to the gilded heights of professional or international football, even if in lesser degree, we are looking at a disaster scene of human endeavour.

There will be a lot of American coaches who have had this experience: you are earning $50,000-$60,000 a year coaching your college team and your college is looking to you for results. So you scour the country for the best available players, and pay them high recruitment money, scholarships, cars and other perquisites. They are a big investment with big reputations. You get them out on the field at the beginning of the season and you begin working them hard, as you are entitled to do. Before you can say snap, some of them are sitting on the sideline with pulled hamstrings or torn tendons. They are likely to be sitting there, eating up college funds and your reputation, for much of the season.

The hamstring or groin injury can last the whole season and the hurt player is always going to be nursing the problem, which makes him less effective than he should be. He is an investment who is not paying off.
    The sudden strickening injury is the worst end-result of unpreparedness. Just as bad is the player who is never really fit to maintain the necessary pace and pressure of the game and is exposing himself more than he needs to damage of the kind that is to some extent inevitable in any physical contact sport.

Early in my talks with United States football coaches, I realised that a lot of the faults were theirs. Even some of the top-paid men did not understand the physiology of exercise in relation to the sport and, consequently, were not giving their expensive stables of players balanced training programmes which would take them over and beyond these injury areas.
    They were working on the theory of German interval training, which states that, as long as you are doing anaerobic training, you can increase your ability to exercise anaerobically. This, we know now, is physiologically incorrect. You can build your oxygen debt capacity to about 15 to 18 litres maximum; if you try to go on from there, the only possible result is a lowering of the body's ability through progressive breakdown.

But this is what the coaches were doing. It was traditional that players came in from their summer vacations and very quickly went into training programmes which included windsprints and other anaerobic exercises for which they were not prepared.

Footballers will argue that football is sprint, sprint, sprint and I will not argue back, but I will argue that the training for it is not just sprint, sprint, sprint. My athletes can sprint but never do until they have developed a high oxygen uptake level which will allow them to sprint easily; or until they have exercised their muscles to withstand the stresses of sprinting. Footballers have to do this, too – and it is even more important when you think that a runner sprints flat-out once in a race without risking physical contact and a footballer may be called on to sprint innumerable times while also taking innumerable knocks and bumps.

Maybe they can get through a succession of twelve hard windsprints before they nearly cross their legs and die. They should be able to do 30. If they cannot, what hope have they when the 25th or 30th need for a windsprint comes up in the course of a game?

The coaches I met did not seem to comprehend this at first. It was foreign to them to be told they had to get their players out, loosen them up, jog them around, build up their oxygen intake levels, exercise their muscular systems, tone their cardio-vascular systems, stretch their tendons and sinews – all before they even thought about sprinting – if they wanted to avoid injuries, get full potential and see ball-handling skills employed to the maximum.

These crippling early season injuries occur because powerful strong muscles are stressed without a preliminary stretching and extending of sinews and tendons.

It is psychologically sound to begin by making the athlete aware of the physical and mechanical reactions of what he is doing. Few athletes, sent out to do something taxing without being given a sound reason for doing it, will put heart and soul into it. Whether you are a gridiron block, a rugby football threequarter, a soccer striker, a league front-row forward or a hockey winger, you are an athlete with the same physiological problems and mechanical behaviour as the miler or sprinter.

Coaching plans can sometimes be made to appear infallible on paper, with a continuous and mathematical development taking place but, invariably, coaches and athletes working this way lack practical knowledge of exercise evaluation and the intensities of exercise that can be applied. Many become obsessed with particular aspects of training and are inclined to emphasise them at the expense of others – endless windsprints, for instance, or non-stop rucking drills.

I have listened to coaches using psychology on their players, assuring them that they cannot lose, that they are in peak form when, in fact, they have not completed a balanced schedule and are physically unprepared for competition. I have known coaches to be more concerned with technique than basic fitness in the belief that superior skills will overcome physical lacks and beat the side that is balanced the other way. But the player skilled in ball-handling but unable to carry it competitively for the duration of a match is a sitting duck for the guy who maybe drops every second pass but is fit enough to catch and beat, every time, the opponent who has got the ball.

I also know athletes who train hard by running big mileages but do not concern themselves with improving their styles of running and so do not gain the full benefit of their long training hours or do not develop their speed or their capacity to exercise anaerobically.

Years of disappointing results can follow when athletes and coaches are guessing instead of carefully balancing their schedules, gaining the best advice available and giving weight to every stage of physiological development. Training for any sport is like putting a jigsaw puzzle together – every piece is necessary if the picture is to be completed and each piece fits only in relation to all the other pieces.

Coaches and athletes cannot just go on following training methods that were successful years before and ignore the evolution of sport. I do not believe there should be revolutionary changes but there must be constant gradual ones as we learn more of the extremes under which the human organism can perform and exercise without loss of improvement and as we gain understanding of the best developmental techniques and how to apply intense training methods.

Many look for quick results and end up using disproportionate amounts of aerobic and anaerobic running. This may not have mattered before we discovered the differences but, now that we do know, you become a menace to your sport and your athletes if you do not apply the knowledge, if you ignore the problems now known to be associated with excessive anaerobic exercise. You then become responsible for retarding the development of the best potential of the athletes you are handling. Anaerobic running and exercise are necessary but their value and use must be clearly understood and properly applied before they can be used successfully.

It is also essential for the modern coach to motivate athletes to maintain conditioning programmes out of season, during vacations, all the time, if they want to succeed.

Happily, this motivation comes easily once you get across the benefits to be obtained from what is a comparatively easy maintenance programme. Out of season, they may not work as hard as they would under a coach's eye but they will do more than they would have done before motivation – and every little bit helps. Even the athlete who is half-hearted is gaining physically on the guy who spreads his shoulders on a sunny beach and leaves them there all day, instead of using the beach for some light running.

The professional footballer in American gridiron or the top ball player stands to be a wealthy man and that should be an incentive to train seriously. But there are other reasons, such as the feeling of going into a new playing season fitter than you have ever been, such as being able easily to absorb techniques and tactics and put them immediately into practice.

Many gridiron players are already great runners and hurdlers – such as Earl MCCULLOUGH, Bob HAYES, Jim HINES and Tommy SMITH. You do not have to strive for their levels in track and field, but you do have to consider that the only way you can hope to compete with them is to do at least some of the conditioning they do.

One small suggestion I made to the coaches: build a ramp with a coconut matting cover, say, 30 to 40 metres long with a 1-in-2 or 1-in-3 grade and get the players to spring up this every day. This is an easy on-the spot adaptation of the hill springing our athletes do to stretch their muscles before they get into speed work. A session just long enough to make the legs feel tired pays remarkable bonuses.

Another: running up steps strengthens the lifting muscles to improve knee lift, increase leg speed and stretch stride length. It particularly helps the vulnerable hamstring group.

These are relatively gentle exercises which rapidly build a basis for tougher training later. It is a lot cheaper to put up the wooden ramp or use grandstand steps than to pay some player big fees and never get to play him because inept conditioning crippled him.

Unlike rugby or league or soccer, in which a man plays all the game, American football keeps taking players off and putting them on. They get breathing spells right out of the game but it remains important to realise that fitness comes mainly from a higher oxygen uptake and, even if a man is going to be on the field only briefly, his concentration and co-ordination are increased by that higher level. The effects of extra oxygen and better-toned blood on the central nervous system sharpen reflexes and enable the player to employ his skills better.

We have proved this many times with golfers who could not improve their scores even if they improved their techniques. We got them jogging fifteen minutes a day and they lowered their handicaps by up to ten strokes because of their improved physical condition, better reflexes and increased co-ordination and concentration.

A coach, given the time and understanding, can develop champions from athletes of ordinary talent. They are developed, not born, though some may have greater natural ability than others. All talents have to be developed through training before their full potential is seen. Many athletes have talents far greater than they imagine – and never find out.

But you have to learn to walk before you can run – to take punishment before you can begin to inflict it on yourself. So, if you have not done so already, go back now and read all of this book. Some of it is specifically aimed at runners; but all of it has significance in some degree to all sportspeople and to all coaches of sportspeople.

Football – or any team field game – is a running sport that requires the individual to have the ability to sprint repeatedly for up to 80 minutes.

Just to run this long at a steady effort requires fine endurance – a high steady state – so obviously to spend it in a series of hard sprints, with physical contacts, sudden stops and starts and changes of direction intermixed, needs equally careful preparation and a high level of fitness.

We are talking now about cardiac efficiency. You can turn it on and off from season to season but you will be only a half-hearted footballer if you do. Real cardiac efficiency comes from easy aerobic running in and out of season, all the year round, to lift your steady state up, increase endurance, reduce the level of oxygen debt incurred for relatively the same workloads and increase the amount of anaerobic exercise you can take without incurring the oxygen debt.

The way it is now, too many footballers lean on the scrum while others do the pushing; take rest periods while others chase the ball; expect the coach to do everything for them in two training sessions; learn to be artful dodgers in play and in practice. It is an imposition on the coach because he cannot pump hard anaerobic exercise into a body that is not aerobically prepared to absorb it. And, if he cannot do that, he cannot be expected at the same time to refine the ball-handling skills, practise plays and tactics and turn out teams that are raring to go and capable of going.

Certainly, as the season progresses, your condition will improve but by then the early games could have been lost and you are probably also on your way to losing form through staleness – the two-bladed physiological/psychological sword that hangs over all inefficient endeavour – because your system is running down, your blood pH is probably low and there is nothing you can do to remedy it except go right back to the basics. The height of the season is not the time for that.

Aerobic conditioning is fully outlined in earlier chapters and, once you have accustomed yourself to a regular regime of running that way, you should aim for a schedule of 30 to 60 minutes a day, regardless of the distance you cover. Always long and short runs, with no more than three longer runs a week. Once you can handle the hour-long run comfortably, you should begin running your miles (kilometres) to the watch. Run over measured courses for a week, without checking your watch as you go and without the influence of another runner, trying to run as evenly in effort and as strongly as your condition allows. By recording the elapsed time, you will have a fair indication of your capacity to train and a basis on which to train further.

In the next week, you use these times for a control over the same courses, only now you check your time for each measured mile (kilometre). If you took an hour to run a 10-mile (16-kilometre) course the first week, you aim now, with due allowance for changes in terrain, to run each of the miles in six minutes (one kilometre in 3 $\frac{3}{4}$ minutes).

When it becomes obvious that the basic times are too slow, lift the average speed for the distance by dropping your mile time to 5.55 or so. This way, you compensate for your improving oxygen uptake level, which is now allowing you to run faster at your near-best aerobic speed. Do not worry if you sometimes slack off. As long as the effort is aerobic, the exercise has value in building cardiac efficiency.

Best results are gained by running about 100 miles (160 kilometres) a week and supplementing this with as many miles as possible at easier efforts. Alternating the run lengths – 10 miles (16 kilometres) today, 20 miles (32 kilometres) tomorrow, rather than 15 miles (24 kilometres) every day – gets the best results. But you, as a footballer, have no need for those distances. That hour a day, or as much as you feel capable of, is your basic requirement; plus, if possible, an easy 15-minute jog at the other end of the day as a supplementary freshener.

During early out-of-season conditioning, there is no need for anaerobic running at all. The ability is dependent on your aerobic capacity and can be developed quickly later as you approach the competitive season. Then, once you are competing, you should take easy runs as often as possible, to maintain oxygen uptake development and help recovery from anaerobic competition and training.

Once you are in this phase, go back and read the section on speed development. There is a concentration here on ankle strength and flexibility which is important, because most footballers are weak and stiff in the ankle. Work at the steep hill springing and step running, and build that knee lift. It not only makes you faster on the field, it makes you more difficult to tackle when you are in full flight.

For real leg speed once you have worked on this programme, find an area that is flat or with a gradual decline about 120-150 metres long. Warm up for about fifteen minutes and then run the course ten times with a three-minute interval between runs and your mind fixed on these objectives:

1. Moving your legs as fast as possible without thinking about stride length.
2. Keeping your upper body as relaxed as possible.
3. Using a normal stride but bringing the knees well up and whippingthose legs through to work the quadriceps hard.

This exercise breaks down muscular viscosity and develops fine speed. Your legs may get tired but if the exercise is maintained it becomes progressively easier and the results come flying through.

Always cool down for about fifteen minutes after the repetitions.

Now go back and read the chapter on anaerobic exercise and its effects on your blood pH. This is important because you must work at a programme that suits you. The same training does not mean similar results; some players will go ahead, some would pull their condition down. It involves dropping the volume of work and increasing the intensity to put the knife-edge on aerobic capacity, without lowering your pH too far, then allowing it to come back up again before you attempt more intense work. It is best to use this type of training only once a week, which brings us to another point a lot of players and coaches do not appreciate.

No hard training should be done within two days of a match. Hard workouts, if you are playing Saturday, should be confined to Monday and Tuesday to give the effects on the blood pH time to recover. Once you are in your playing season, hard training is necessary only to improve your playing condition. Continual hard exercise, in which a lot of footballers still indulge, is a mistake. You need now to stay fresh and sharp and you have no hope of doing that while you are constantly at hard repetition training. You may do one or the other well, but never both.

Here is a guideline to a ball player's running schedule:

Beginning eighteen weeks before season opens –

Monday: Half an hour strongly over hills, weights training
Tuesday: One hour steady
Wednesday: Half an hour strongly over hills, weights training
Thursday: One hour steady
Friday: Rest, weights training
Saturday: One hour steady
Sunday: Half an hour easy fartlek

The three long runs are the nucleus of the conditioning schedule; the other days are used for running over undulating terrain to condition the leg muscles against uphill and downhill pressures.

Beginning twelve weeks before season opens –

Monday: Half an hour of hill springing and steep hill running, weights training
Tuesday: One hour steady
Wednesday: Leg speed running over 120 metres, up to 10 times with 3-minute jogging intervals, weights training
Thursday: One hour steady
Friday: Rest, weights training
Saturday: Half an hour of hill springing and hill running
Sunday: One hour steady

During this period, the leg speed running is incorporated to begin to overcome muscle viscosity and improve muscular reactions.

Beginning eight weeks before season opens –

Monday: Up to an hour fartlek, weights training
Tuesday: Football training or anaerobic repetitions (i.e. 200 metres x 10 times with 200 metres jogging intervals)
Wednesday: Forwards – up to one hour fartlek, weights training; backs – sprint training, weights training

Thursday: Football training or anaerobic repetitions
Friday: Rest, weights training
Saturday: Football training or anaerobic repetitions
Sunday: Leg speed over 120 metres x ten times

While you are, in this period, developing your anaerobic capacity to exercise, you must also find time to keep the volume running going. The football training is rough and tumble play for contact conditioning and to work at fundamentals and combination training.

Season begins –

Monday: Jog up to an hour, weights training
Tuesday: Football training, including 100 metres windsprints
Wednesday: Easy fartlek or sprint training, weights training
Thurday: Football training
Friday: Rest
Saturday: Play
Sunday: Light jog

Footballer must train to play well, but they must keep fresh and sharp for a long period so avoid anaerobic training on Thursday and Fridays. The Thursday session can be fast but there should be no remorseless grind into exhaustion. For example: back movements for combination training, forward dribbling and passing movements, tactical plays.

These schedules are strictly a guide for balanced training. If you carried through this programme intelligently, there could be no question of your overall fitness and ability to improve markedly. But this is an ultimate schedule. You might not want or be able to train all through the off-season; so when you do start, you should aim to run all the aerobic miles you can before your coach commits you to the rigours of team session training.

Or you can train all through the off-season to a lesser mileage than suggested, as long as you maintain the proportional balance indicated. Do not, for instance, concentrate only on weights and build a big muscular system without the cardiac efficiency to go with it. Nor is there a lot of point in doing a lot of running without adding the muscle build-up. That might be fine for runners but footballers need a blend of both.

You can do too little or too much, you can do it too intensively or too casually – and you could be wasting a lot of time and effort. Think about it carefully and get an even balance and stick with that and you should be all right.

Even if you cut the schedule in half, you will be working along the right lines. If you got really lazy and jogged only fifteen minutes every other day until you began normal team training, you would still benefit. It just depends, does not it, on how good you want to be.

Now let us look at weights training and strength. Muscular strength is simply the ability to exert a single explosive force against an object. Because football is a contact sport, you need to condition your muscular system generally to develop strong supple muscles capable of acting quickly and withstanding the hard contacts of a full game.

The muscles on which you concentrate depend on the type of football you play and the position you occupy in the team but it benefits all players to go through a general strengthening programme. This is something that, initially, has to be done under the guidance of an experienced coach and should always be done regularly. This avoids the risk that you could develop one group of muscles in imbalance with other groups, which could be detrimental.

How you exercise those muscles is important, too, and here are some observations made by Professor M. HOWELL, of Canada, relating to experiments conducted by MUELLER and HETTINGER, two internationally recognised weights-training experts:

The maximum training effect is achieved by using only 40 to 50 percent of the maximum strength in voluntary isometric muscular contractions.

Strength neither increases nor decreases when only 20 to 30 percent of strength is used; losses occur when less than 20 percent is used.

Maintaining a maximum isometric contraction for only two seconds is sufficient to provide a training stimulus; when only two-thirds maximum strength is used, it should be maintained for four to six seconds and so on.

The maximum increase is obtained with one training stimulus a day and several maximum contractions one after the other do not increase strength any faster.

When training sessions are held every second day, the increase in strength is about 80 percent of the daily gain: with two sessions a week, about 60 percent; once a week, about 40 percent. One stimulus every fourteen days produces no changes at all.

As a guide here is a schedule to be used in relation to your current fitness level, individual strength and capacity to exercise. In these exercises, a set is a period of exercise in which a number of repetitions are done without setting the weights down. A set can be any number of repetitions but in your first workout you should perform only one set of each exercise and gradually increase.

Individual strengths vary widely, so we cannot set standard starting poundages but if you begin with weights you can comfortably raise ten times in succession you should be right. Alternate the exercises between upper-body and lower-body effects to spread the effort evenly.

1. Two-arm barbell military press – approx. starting poundage (ASP) of 22, 25, 27 kg. Three sets, three to five repetitions. Concentrate on fast explosive-type presses rather than slow deliberate movements.
2. Biceps curl – ASP 18, 20, 22 kg. Three sets, ten reps.
3. Full squats with barbell on shoulders – ASP 32, 36, 40 kg. Three sets, ten to twelve reps. Concentrate on straight back, head up and a fairly fast drive. Go down until the thighs are parallel with the floor. Can be performed flat-footed, with heels on a 5 to 7 cm block or you can go right up on your toes each time.
4. Jump squats with dum-bells held at sides – ASP 9, 11, 13 kg. Three sets, fifteen reps.
5. Two-arm dumbell prone press on bench – ASP 7, 9, 11 kg. Three sets, eight to ten reps. Concentrate on a fast type of press.
6. Sit-ups – start without weights. Three sets, ten to fifteen reps. Begin lying flat on floor; later use an inclined board with foot straps; than add 1 kg weight held behind the neck.
7. Two-arm barbell clean and jerk – ASP 36, 40, 45 kg. Three sets, two to four reps. For overall strength, co-ordination and timing.

8. Chin-ups – two or three sets of what you are capable of. Palms of hands facing away. Repeat with palms facing as a separate exercise.
9. Finger flips off a wall – three sets, ten to fifteen reps. Lock the arms and use the fingers only.
10. Finger push-ups off the floor – three sets, ten to fifteen reps. Start on finger-tips, push with straight back.

If you do three sessions a week, increase the weights according to reactions and progress, by 2 to 4 $\frac{1}{2}$ kg a week. Have the sessions on alternate days, not on consecutive days.

Rest a minute between sets and three minutes between exercises. Record carefully what you do and what weight increases you make.

Two weeks before the season opens, reduce weights sessions to two a week, then to one a week when you begin playing and have them early in the week.

These are the fundamentals. You and a weights-training coach should look at your basic weaknesses and individual needs and work on them in conjunction.

Many football clubs now have weights-training equipment or have linked up with a gymnasium. Those that have not would be making a better investment of club funds in providing gym facilities rather than a plush bar for members, supporters and free-loaders.

If you cannot get at proper weights, you can compromise. Here is one simple exercise that will strengthen every muscle, including some you never knew you had: get a yard of loose metal, put it where you can shovel it to another site one day and shovel it back again the next.

A piece of pipe with a bag of sand at each end, a resistant-spring exerciser, two plastic bottles, the type with handles, filled with sand – all are inexpensive weights-training aids. If you have the will, you will find the way.

The programme we have set out here is basically the same wherever you play in the team, whatever game your team plays. Specialty exercises come in during the last ten weeks or so of the programme.

For instance, if you are going to be a quarter back or rugby five-eighth or stand-off half, you have to learn to move your body a yard before anyone else moves an inch. You are going to be a quick, short, sharp sprinter because, if you can really burst for ten to twenty metres, you are going to get through.

Years ago when I was training for rugby, we would stand facing a wall with our backs to a mark maybe fifteen metres away. The coach would blow a whistle and we would turn and sprint for the mark. Then we would walk back again and, at some point, the coach would whistle again and, zip, we would spin and sprint back. We did this perhaps 20, 30, or 40 times. If we were fit enough, it really sharpened us.

We would give our backs good sprint training, make them really run, weave them through markers like a slalom to get sidestepping and weaving built into their sprinting. This is what speed training and co-ordination is all about.

Rugby forwards need a lot of windsprints, even more than many of the backs because they are going to be doing them continually in a game. They should work on them for four to six weeks. The average forward is a big man, but he also has to be a fast man these days.

New Zealand, though it has been at the top of the rugby tree for most of the years since World War Two, has always suffered from a lack of real speed. I have seen it when we played British teams. The British players have such leg speed they do not have to break through the New Zealand line; they just run round it, getting away because of that vital first yard of fast movement.

One of our greatest postwar forwards, Kel TREMAIN proved the point every time he played but most coaches did not see it. Kel trained every day out of season and ran up to 160 kilometres a week to condition himself to play football. He was always where the ball was or was going to be and he was still going at the end of the game when others were down on their knees. He scored a lot of tries in the last quarters of matches because he prepared himself to play 80 minutes.

Colin and Stan MEADS were the same. They were farmers and ran all over their properties to do their work and keep fit.

Whatever your sport, you can use a light running and weights programme to play it better. The jogging that can improve golfers can do the same for canoeists, rackets players, billiards players, yachtsmen, rowers, anyone at all. All it needs is fifteen minutes a day.

Weights training can be adapted to any sport that calls for specific hitting, striking, throwing or other actions. Simply fill two plastic bottles (with handles) with sand and hold one in each hand while you go through the actions you follow in your particular sport. The serving, forehand and backhand of tennis can be improved by adding this resistance. The golfer's swing gains. Same with badminton, squash, table tennis.

Hang the bottles on your toes for leg strengthening; go through a stretching and suppling routine with them. The effort is light, the results excellent.

No programme is needed. All you have to do is consider which muscles you use specifically in your sport and then work at them with your improvised weights, as and when you feel like it. Use a short session to warm up for and wind down from your regular jog. For remarkably little effort, you will get a lot more satisfaction and enjoyment from your sport.

Uphill running, driving hard off the back foot, gives the quads a vital fall workout.

Our Programme